"Brother Yun is fervent and fiery for Jesus. I am sure that he will be among the Lord's anointed of the next generation, who build the kingdom of God in the toughest places on earth. I appreciate and honor this great servant of God."

—Reinhard Bonnke, German evangelist and founder of Christ for All Nations

"Brother Yun's life is one so totally captured by Jesus that no imaginable hardship or persecution can stop him from being more than a conqueror."

—Rolland and Heidi Baker, missionaries to Africa and directors of Iris Ministries

Living Water

Powerful teachings from the international
bestselling author of *The Heavenly Man*

BROTHER YUN

EDITED BY PAUL HATTAWAY

ZONDERVAN®

ZONDERVAN.com/
AUTHORTRACKER
follow your favorite authors

Living Water

Copyright © 2008 by Brother Yun and Paul Hattaway

Requests for information should be addressed to:

Zondervan, *Grand Rapids, Michigan* 49530

Library of Congress Cataloging-in-Publication Data

Yun, Brother, 1958-
     Living water / Brother Yun ; edited by Paul Hattaway.
       p. cm.
     ISBN   978-0-310-28554-0 (softcover)
     1. Christian life. I. Hattaway, Paul, 1968- II. Title.
   BV4501.3.Y86 2008
   248.4–dc22

                                 2008007383

Internet addresses (websites, blogs, etc.) and telephone numbers printed in this book are offered as a resource to you. These are not intended in any way to be or imply an endorsement on the part of Zondervan, nor do we vouch for the content of these sites and numbers for the life of this book.

Where numerals are spelled out, the publisher has used American style.

Interior design by Christine Orejuela-Winkelman

Printed in the United States of America

08 09 10 11 12 13 14 • 20 19 18 17 16 15 14 13 12 11 10 9 8 7 6 5 4 3 2 1

On the last and greatest day of the Feast, Jesus stood and said in a loud voice, "If anyone is thirsty, let him come to me and drink. Whoever believes in me, as the Scripture has said, streams of living water will flow from within him." By this he meant the Spirit, whom those who believed in him were later to receive.

John 7:37–39

Contents

Part Three
Soldiers for Christ

Introduction

Brother Yun's testimony, recorded in *The Heavenly Man*, has deeply impacted the lives of hundreds of thousands of Christians around the world since its publication in 2002. It is a joy for me now to be invited to play a small part in bringing you this companion volume, *Living Water*.

In 1997 Brother Yun left China at the insistence of fellow believers there. That began his ministry to people all over the world. Since that time he has shared in more than 1,000 meetings in nations throughout Africa, Asia, North America, the Middle East and the South Pacific, as well as almost every country in Europe. He speaks of Christ's love and His call for wholehearted commitment in such a compelling way that many people have been blessed and transformed wherever God has allowed Yun to go.

When I reflect on my personal experience of Brother Yun's ministry, I think of his living model of what it means to remain truly humble. I see him willing to serve any person he encounters without the slightest hesitancy or reserve. Yun shares the Word of God just as passionately in large meetings with thousands of people as he does in small Bible studies with a few individuals. He consistently shies away from any desire for celebrity or the public praise of men. Yun can often be found staying for hours to pray with those who come forward after he speaks. He does not merely say a few words and move on; he takes a genuine interest in each person. He gives them his full attention, just as Jesus did. On many occasions I've seen Yun kneel down and ask the people in the prayer line to pray for him.

It is extraordinary for me to witness Brother Yun's unconquerable ability to win people to Jesus. Some people believed he would struggle to have the same kind of impact outside China as he had before he left his homeland. However, whenever I travel with him in the Western world, I am constantly amazed at the number of people he introduces to Christ. Whether at airports or restaurants or in hotel lobbies, I frequently find Yun kneeling on the floor and praying with a tear-filled individual who is opening his heart to the Lord.

Occasionally, I step back and try to analyze the difference between his soul-winning methods and those commonly employed by most Western Christians. I have come to realize that it has nothing to do with methodology at all, but everything to do with relationship. Yun walks closely with Jesus Christ, and it is natural for that intimacy to spill over to others around him. Non-Christians are often attracted to the gospel because they feel God's love and presence pouring out through Brother Yun.

Many people have been stirred and awakened by *The Heavenly Man*. Very few of those people will ever have the opportunity to hear Brother Yun in person. *Living Water* has been prepared for exactly such people. It records a selection of the most inspirational and challenging messages Yun has shared over the past decade.

Because of the familiarity of Chinese Christians with the harshest of persecutions, they tend to have a different perspective from most Western-trained teachers. Yun's fresh application of the Scriptures may well bring many readers to a deeper walk with Jesus. His call to discipleship will offer them a different vision of their work for God's kingdom.

This volume is arranged in three parts.

- Part 1, "Freedom in Christ," contains messages relating to the spiritual life of the believer, particularly the need to remove all that can potentially block our relationship with God. These foundational principles lay the essential groundwork for the later chapters.
- Part 2, "Streams of Living Water," is about equipping believers for service in God's kingdom. Brother Yun teaches God's requirements for surrender, obedience and sacrifice and shows that His kingdom advances through human weakness rather than human strength. Yun takes readers graciously by the hand and shows them how living water can flow from within every Christian, bringing refreshment to many thirsty souls.
- Part 3, "Soldiers for Christ," explains the obstacles and storms disciples are likely to encounter in their lives. However, Brother Yun shows that such hardships actually aid Christians in their spiritual journey. These insights are drawn from Yun's personal experience enduring torture and pain for the sake of the gospel. Despite his harsh experiences, Yun's life and ministry are marked by infectious joy, zeal for God and love for his fellow man. How this can be the case in spite of all he has undergone will provide tender but practical encouragement.

Within these messages, *Living Water* includes many accounts from Yun's personal life. He openly shares his struggles, and he's frank about the long process of refining and shaping through which God has led him. Yun's teaching, therefore, carries the ring of authenticity. The reader will recognize the voice of one who has gone through what he speaks about, and not someone who is merely passing on lessons learned from a textbook.

Brother Yun spent decades in China in the midst of the revival fires. He has seen God move in ways that many of us can only imagine. Yet he often grieves to see among God's people a lack of obedience and a loss of true zeal for God. From a spirit of love and humility, Yun shares principles the Lord has taught him. He desires to offer each person and each church the very experience he has known of the streams of living water that are promised to all who believe in Jesus Christ.

I pray that *Living Water* will bring relief to millions of Christians whose walk with God has become dry and barren. The source of living water is undeniably found in Jesus Christ alone.

Paul Hattaway

Part 1

Freedom in Christ

Repentance

"Those whom I love I rebuke and discipline. So be earnest, and repent."

Revelation 3:19

One of the greatest missionaries to China in the twentieth century was a single Norwegian woman named Marie Monsen. Although I was not even born when she ministered throughout my home province of Henan, I heard many stories from elderly brothers and sisters who knew her and were blessed by her ministry.

Marie Monsen was a Lutheran missionary, but her fervency and uncompromising message frequently put her at odds with her missionary society. Church leaders told me how much Monsen loved the Chinese people, especially the family of God, and how she was willing to do whatever was necessary to serve Jesus. In those days (the 1920s and '30s), life was extremely difficult for foreign missionaries in China. They had to contend with terrible opposition everywhere they went, mobs of bandits roaming the countryside and a devastating civil war.

Monsen had one main message that she preached everywhere she went. She taught that to be a follower of Christ, a person has to first thoroughly repent of their sins. By that she didn't simply mean that people must confess their sins and ask forgiveness. That was only the first step. She meant that their whole lives, desires, motives and plans must be surrendered to God. Each Christian must die to self and completely hand their past, present and future over to the Lord Jesus Christ. One of her favorite Bible passages was Romans 12:1–2:

> I urge you, brothers, in view of God's mercy, to offer your bodies as living sacrifices, holy and pleasing to God—this is your spiritual act of worship. Do not conform any longer to the pattern of this world, but be transformed by the renewing of your mind. Then you will be able to test and approve what God's will is—his good, pleasing and perfect will.

On occasions the holy anger of God came upon Marie Monsen, and she often convicted her fellow missionaries and the Chinese church leaders of their lukewarm commitment and secret sins. Many were told they were hypocrites, and Monsen was never afraid to set forth the standard of God's holiness. Monsen frequently asked missionaries if they had ever really experienced a rebirth in Christ and if they had completely surrendered their lives to Him. This must have come as a shock to many missionaries who, it was supposed, had forsaken all to serve Christ on the other side of the world. More than a few of them, however, were convicted by the searching light of the Holy Spirit and could not confidently say that they had ever been converted. Monsen led a number of her fellow missionaries into a personal relationship with Jesus.

Because most of the Henan Christians in the pre-Communism era had been so strongly challenged to thoroughly repent and be in right relationship with God, they were able to better withstand the storms of persecution that buffeted the Chinese church throughout the 1950s, '60s and '70s. I have heard countless stories of men and women who sacrificed their lives as martyrs for Jesus during this time. One pastor had a noose placed around his neck and was made to stand atop three tables stacked on top of each other. The pastor's wife, children and extended family were all called to the police station to witness the scene. The officers gruffly declared, "You have two options! Either you choose to continue believing in Jesus, or you deny Jesus. Make your choice now!"

The aged pastor looked down into the eyes of his beloved family, but he knew what he must do. He calmly announced, "Even if you cut off my head and my blood covers the ground, I will never deny Jesus."

Immediately the officers kicked the legs of the bottom table, causing the structure to collapse. In an instant the noose tightened and the pastor went to be with Jesus Christ forever.

Due to the example of many God-fearing people like this, the church in my province, which had numbered only in the tens of thousands of believers prior to 1949, today numbers in the millions. Disciples from Henan have been sent out all over China as ambassadors of the good news.

As I have traveled around the world, I have come to realize that the kind of message Marie Monsen and other missionaries preached in China is much needed today. Repentance is a foundational key to the Christian life, but in many places it has been a neglected doctrine. In countless churches today, preachers have watered down their message so that it does not bear much resemblance to the gospel as outlined in the Scriptures.

Instead of people hearing that God's kingdom is available to all those who are willing to forsake the world and wholeheartedly follow Jesus, thousands of sermons are preached every Sunday in which Jesus is presented as a Savior only, but not as Lord and Master. People are told "Jesus will help you, bless you, forgive you and empower you." But very little is said about repentance, humility and sacrifice.

You see, we are all called to run a race for Jesus, and repentance is the starting line of that race. It's futile to try to run the race if you never made it to the starting line to begin with! This is the problem with many believers today. They are trying to follow the Lord, but they have never truly repented and surrendered their lives to Jesus Christ. The result of the false gospel so prevalent today can be seen in churches full of halfhearted Christians whose lives are still centered on selfishness and the principles of the world.

Jesus came to bring the kingdom of God to the earth. He came to completely transform individuals, families and nations from the inside out—a radical revolution that would change the world through obedient, blood-bought servants who are willing to bow their knee and say, "Lord, after all You have done for me, what would You have me do for You?"

Jesus told the church in Laodicea, "I know your deeds, that you are neither cold nor hot. I wish you were either one or the other! So, because you are lukewarm—neither hot nor cold—I am about to spit you out of my mouth" (Rev. 3:15–16). This message from the resurrected Lord must have been an awful shock to the Laodicean Christians! They were well-off, comfortable and self-sufficient. They probably thought that Jesus was proud of their achievements and appreciative of their pious acts. Instead of patting them on the back, however, Jesus exposed the reality of their spiritually diseased condition:

"You say, 'I am rich; I have acquired wealth and do not need a thing.' But you do not realize that you are wretched, pitiful, poor, blind and naked. I counsel you to buy from me gold refined in the fire, so you can become rich; and white clothes to wear, so you can cover your shameful nakedness; and salve to put on your eyes, so you can see."

Revelation 3:17–18

Why did Jesus say these harsh words? Did He hate the Laodicean believers? Certainly not! In fact, His motivation—as always—was one of love, tough love. He loved the Laodiceans so much that He could not sit idly and let them perish in their sin and selfishness. "Those whom I love I rebuke and discipline. So be earnest, and repent" (Rev. 3:19).

Repentance is both the first step to walking in the kingdom of God and the key to continuing in a place of obedience and submission to the Lord. The very first message Jesus proclaimed in His ministry was, "Repent, for the kingdom of heaven is near" (Matt. 4:17). Without a deep experience of repentance in our lives, we will continually struggle with basic sin and never mature as believers.

The Devil doesn't care if you have served the Lord in the past. What makes him frightened is if you are living for Jesus Christ *today*, relying on and trusting Him right *now*, and being willing to obey the leading of the Holy Spirit.

We may look like we belong in the kingdom of God, and we may be successful in tricking other people, but the all-knowing God cannot be fooled. We have to submit to Jesus as Lord and King if we want to dwell in His kingdom. We cannot trick God, whose "solid foundation stands firm, sealed with this inscription: 'The Lord knows those who are his,' and,

'Everyone who confesses the name of the Lord must turn away from wickedness'" (2 Tim. 2:19).

Jesus longs to have us all at His wedding banquet, but we cannot enter if we continue to live according to the principles of the world. The parable of the wedding banquet says:

> *"When the king came in to see the guests, he noticed a man there who was not wearing wedding clothes. 'Friend,' he asked, 'how did you get in here without wedding clothes?' The man was speechless. Then the king told the attendants, 'Tie him hand and foot, and throw him outside, into the darkness, where there will be weeping and gnashing of teeth.' For many are invited, but few are chosen."*
>
> *Matthew 22:11–14*

God knows who is a citizen of His kingdom and who is an impostor. If we have received an invitation to the wedding feast of the kingdom of God, we must wear the clothes that He tells us to, and not our own. We must accept His Word and live by it, aligning our lifestyle and choices to match the commands of the King. This is repentance.

Repentance is such an integral part of Christian life. In fact, without repentance it is impossible to live in the kingdom of God. Living with one foot in God's kingdom and one foot in the world is no different than an unfaithful spouse with two lovers. James put it quite bluntly: "You adulterous people, don't you know that friendship with the world is hatred toward God? Anyone who chooses to be a friend of the world becomes an enemy of God. Or do you think Scripture says without reason that the spirit he caused to live in us envies intensely?" (James 4:4–5).

John similarly wrote, "Do not love the world or anything in the world. If anyone loves the world, the love of the Father is not in him. For everything in the world – the cravings of sinful man, the lust of his eyes and the boasting of what he has and does – comes not from the Father but from the world. The world and its desires pass away, but the man who does the will of God lives forever" (1 John 2:15–17).

One day we will all stand before the judgment seat of Christ and be required to account for our lives. Now is the time to repent, before it is too late! "In the past God overlooked such ignorance, but now he commands all people everywhere to repent. For he has set a day when he will judge the world with justice by the man he has appointed. He has given proof of this to all men by raising him from the dead" (Acts 17:30–31).

Dear friend, if you sense the conviction of the Holy Spirit tugging at your conscience, then fall on your knees and cry out to God from a repentant heart. Ask the Holy Spirit to take full control of your life and to help you daily walk in humility and dependence on Him.

*L*essons from *E*sau

> "I am coming soon. Hold on to what you have, so that no one will take your crown. Him who overcomes I will make a pillar in the temple of my God. Never again will he leave it. I will write on him the name of my God and the name of the city of my God, the new Jerusalem, which is coming down out of heaven from my God; and I will also write on him my new name. He who has an ear, let him hear what the Spirit says to the churches ...
>
> "Those whom I love I rebuke and discipline. So be earnest, and repent."
>
> *Revelation 3:11–13, 19*

*F*or all those who follow Jesus Christ, God has promised a beautiful future both in this life and in eternity. Your life in this world may be hard and full of difficulties, but it is nevertheless beautiful and abundant, for Jesus said, "I have come that they may have life, and have it to the full" (John 10:10).

As we walk through this world, however, we must be very careful to protect the inheritance God has given us. "Hold on to what you have," Jesus told the church in Philadelphia, "so that no one will take your crown" (Rev. 3:11). The child of God must always "watch and pray so that you will not fall into temptation. The spirit is willing, but the body is weak" (Mark 14:38).

On certain occasions in my life, I have failed to walk in the circumspect manner that God requires, and I have allowed self-confidence to enter my heart and usurp my dependence on God.

In 2001 I was imprisoned in Myanmar (Burma) because I was too confident in my own abilities, and my flesh rose up and smothered my spiritual perception. I disobeyed the Lord and was sent to prison for seven years. I shed many tears of repentance over my pride and stupidity, and as a result, the Lord had mercy on me and I was released after just seven months and seven days of confinement.

God has promised a bright future to all who follow His Son, but over the years my heart has been pierced with grief as I have witnessed many servants of the Lord compromise their witness through sin and affection to the world. Tragically, many have lost their inheritance and subverted the plans God had laid out for them.

There are also many people in the Bible whose failed lives serve as a warning to us. These men and women also had received a beautiful future from God, but they lost their inheritance.

The story of Esau is tragic. He was the firstborn son, a skillful hunter and the apple of his father's eye. The most precious thing Esau possessed was his birthright. Being the oldest son, he would be in charge of the household when his father died, and he would assume the role of priest in his family, leading them to worship God. Despite such a wonderful and bright future, the Bible says that Esau *"despised his birthright"* (Gen. 25:34, emphasis added). His deceptive brother, Jacob, with his mother acting as an accomplice, was easily able to tempt Esau, who traded in his inheritance for a miserable bowl of lentil stew. The Bible records the sorry account:

> *Once when Jacob was cooking some stew, Esau came in from the open country, famished. He said to Jacob, "Quick, let me have some of that red stew! I'm famished!"....*
>
> *Jacob replied, "First sell me your birthright."*
>
> *"Look, I am about to die," Esau said. "What good is the birthright to me?"*
>
> *But Jacob said, "Swear to me first." So he swore an oath to him, selling his birthright to Jacob.*
>
> *Then Jacob gave Esau some bread and some lentil stew. He ate and drank, and then got up and left.*
>
> *Genesis 25:29–34*

Before you rush to judgment on how stupid and disrespectful Esau was to despise his birthright, consider all those times you have disobeyed the Lord. Tragically, there are thousands of men and women of God today—some of whom once had powerful ministries that operated in the anointing and favor of God—who have traded in their inheritance for a bowl of stew.

To Esau, the bowl of stew represented something that could meet the immediate needs of his flesh. The Bible says he was "famished." Many others have shipwrecked their faith and destroyed their witness for the Lord by giving in to their fleshly needs through sexual impurity, mishandling of finances and a host of other sins.

There may be a bowl of stew in your life as well. If you make a wrong decision and partake of it, it can destroy your life and bring you untold misery and pain. Consider Esau,

Adam and Eve, Samson, Solomon, Judas or Ananias and Sapphira, just to name a few. If you have been a Christian for any length of time, you too will know of believers who have turned their backs on God and despised their birthright.

The last mention of Esau in the Bible was made by the writer of Hebrews, who told us, "See to it that no one misses the grace of God and that no bitter root grows up to cause trouble and defile many. See that no one is sexually immoral, or is godless like Esau, who for a single meal sold his inheritance rights as the oldest son. Afterward, as you know, when he wanted to inherit this blessing, he was rejected. He could bring about no change of mind, though he sought the blessing with tears" (12:15–17).

Dear Christian, it is interesting that the above verse mentions sexual immorality along with Esau's sin. There have been far too many Christians willing to exchange their birthright for a moment of sexual pleasure, and like Esau, they have been unable to gain back that which they willfully gave away. The Proverbs warn us of the consequences of adultery in no uncertain terms: "A man who commits adultery lacks judgment; whoever does so destroys himself. Blows and disgrace are his lot, and his shame will never be wiped away" (6:32–33).

Too many Christians, and even preachers, have lacked a proper fear of God and have paid too much attention to money, fame and sex. As a result, they have lost the bright future God promised them. My heart has often grieved when I've seen the devastation such sin has brought to parents, spouses, children and other members of the body of Christ.

Satan is an expert at tempting us to fall. He knows that if he can attract us with something we can touch, feel or taste, other things become less important than satisfying these senses.

Satan tempted Adam and Eve's senses, and they succumbed. He also tempted Jesus through his senses, but our Lord overcame the Devil's wiles. Hallelujah! For "we do not have a high priest who is unable to sympathize with our weaknesses, but we have one who has been tempted in every way, just as we are—yet was without sin. Let us then approach the throne of grace with confidence, so that we may receive mercy and find grace to help us in our time of need" (Heb. 4:15–16).

People can become controlled by their lust, which causes them to make ignorant and wrong decisions. They ultimately pay a very heavy price for their indiscretions. Many people have told me how they wish they would have known the consequences of an action they took, which destroyed their marriages, broke their families and brought untold misery to their lives.

Thankfully, God has provided a way for His children so we don't have to be overcome by fleshly temptations. One of the fruits of the Spirit is self-control. This doesn't mean that we control ourselves, but it means we must submit to the Holy Spirit who lives inside of us and who helps us to fear God and hate sin.

There is an important truth that I think many Christians have not properly grasped: it is *only* the grace of God that can help and train us to overcome temptation. Paul told Titus that "the grace of God that brings salvation has appeared to all men. It teaches us to say 'No' to ungodliness and worldly passions, and to live self-controlled, upright and godly lives in this present age, while we wait for the blessed hope—the glorious appearing of our great God and Savior, Jesus Christ" (Titus 2:11–13).

Some Christians think they can conquer their fleshly desires and temptations by their own willpower and strength.

Some are even willing to go to great lengths in that battle, but if your struggle does not draw its strength from the grace of God, it will likely be in vain. Note what the apostle Paul wrote to the Christians at Colosse: "Since you died with Christ to the basic principles of this world, why, as though you still belonged to it, do you submit to its rules: 'Do not handle! Do not taste! Do not touch!'? These are all destined to perish with use, because they are based on human commands and teachings. Such regulations indeed have an appearance of wisdom, with their self-imposed worship, their false humility and their harsh treatment of the body, but they lack any value in restraining sensual indulgence" (Col. 2:20–23).

Not only can an individual Christian lose their way and ruin their God-given inheritance, but churches and even whole nations can, and do, fall. On several occasions God punished Israel because of their sin and disobedience. Even in their deepest despair, under the correction of God, there was hope for Israel. And there is hope for you if you have lost your way. Jeremiah was despised by the people because he spoke messages that the people didn't want to hear. He prophesied judgment and captivity while all the other prophets were declaring peace and prosperity. When the Babylonians came and took God's people away into slavery, however, his message must have started to ring true to the stubborn-hearted nation.

Even in their darkest hour, God offered a glimmer of hope to His crushed people. The following verse is often quoted in part, but we need to understand the context it was used in. Jeremiah prophesied, "This is what the LORD says: 'When seventy years are completed for Babylon, I will come to you and fulfill my gracious promise to bring you back to this place. For I know the plans I have for you,' declares the LORD, 'plans to prosper you and not to harm you, plans to give you hope and a future. Then you will call upon me and come and pray to me, and I will listen to you'" (Jer. 29:10–12).

After being delivered from Egypt, the children of Israel were required to follow the pillar of cloud and the pillar of fire through the wilderness. When it moved, they were to move, and when it stopped, they were to stop. They were not to fall behind, and they were not to go ahead. While they remained with God's presence, they received His protection, direction and provision. If a person foolishly wandered off into the desert by himself and got separated from God's people, he would not last long. The desert was full of poisonous snakes and scorpions and totally devoid of water and food. The manna and quail that fell from heaven only fell on the camp where God's people dwelled; it did not fall everywhere in the desert. The water that gushed from the rock at Kadesh satisfied the people who were camped there. If someone was straggling far behind in the desert, it would not be of any use to them.

Perhaps you have lost track of God's plan for your life. Perhaps you have wandered off track and have spent years trying to relocate the pillar of fire and cloud. Your spiritual provision has dried up, and your life has been constantly under attack from dangerous and destructive forces. If this is your experience, then I have good news! There is a way back.

The way back starts by thoroughly repenting and denouncing the sin and disobedience that caused you to wander away in the first place. Stop trying to manage your own life, and realize you will continue to fail until you truly submit to the lordship of Jesus Christ. Stop doing your will, and start obeying God's will. Acknowledge your total dependence on Him, and He will show you the right pathway in the desert, one that will lead you back to the camp of God's children. Jesus will embrace you again, for He has promised, "All that the Father gives me will come to me, and whoever comes to me I will never drive away" (John 6:37).

For those who have faithfully followed the Lord and have not strayed from the camp, thank God for His faithfulness and mercy, and continue to walk circumspectly, realizing that your flesh is a cunning enemy that is always seeking a way to deceive you. Don't arrogantly think for a second that your own gifts and abilities have helped you walk with Jesus, because it is only through His abundant grace that you can stand. Paul encouraged and admonished the church at Philippi with these words: "Therefore, my dear friends, as you have always obeyed – not only in my presence, but now much more in my absence – continue to work out your salvation with fear and trembling, for it is God who works in you to will and to act according to his good purpose" (Phil. 2:12–13).

Dear brothers and sisters, as a fellow pilgrim I ask you to obey and follow the Lord, live a godly life and finish the race that God has called you to, regardless of whatever pain, difficulties, struggles, temptations and trials you may meet on the journey. Be "confident of this, that he who began a good work in you will carry it on to completion until the day of Christ Jesus" (Phil. 1:6).

Be strong in the Lord, don't forsake God's principles and "do not throw away your confidence; it will be richly rewarded. You need to persevere so that when you have done the will of God, you will receive what he has promised" (Heb. 10:35–36).

Forgiveness
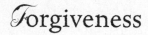

Out of the depths I cry to you, O Lord;
O Lord, hear my voice.
Let your ears be attentive
to my cry for mercy.
If you, O Lord, kept a record of sins,
O Lord, who could stand?
But with you there is forgiveness;
therefore you are feared.

Psalm 130:1–4

Have you ever been treated unjustly? Has someone hurt you without cause?

Unless you have been living in an isolated cave all your life, the answer to these questions will surely be yes.

The world is full of bitterness and unforgiveness. It could be said that whole spiritual and political structures are founded and based on bitterness.

There is just one solution to the threat of terrorism in the world today. Military power will never solve the problem, for you cannot overcome a spiritual disease with guns and bombs. The only hope is for a genuine God-sent revival to sweep millions of people into the kingdom of God, changing individuals from the inside out and replacing hate with love, and bitterness with forgiveness. The living water of Jesus can enter communities where terrorism is fostered, bringing new life and hope through the cross of Jesus Christ.

As I have traveled around the world meeting numerous Christians, I have become aware that many have long struggled to forgive other people who have wronged them. I believe it is only through relationship with Jesus Christ that we can start to walk in the freedom that comes from a life of forgiveness.

Unforgiveness soon becomes bitterness, and nothing will choke the streams of living water that are meant to flow from your life more than a root of bitterness. The root can grow so large that a person's whole personality is twisted and deformed by it.

The first step for anyone to become whole in Christ is to accept responsibility for their own sins and failures. There is no point in blaming anyone else, regardless of what terrible things have happened to us. When someone hurts us, our natural response is to pull back and withdraw. We are created in such a way that we want to avoid pain. But then something takes place that requires us to make a vital decision. When we pull back from a person who has caused us pain, we must decide whether or not to let bitterness into our heart.

Bitterness is what happens to you when you will not forgive. Bitterness is to hold on to an injustice that has been done to you. The Bible indicates that when a Christian is destroyed by bitterness, it not only ruins them, but it ruins other people as well: "See to it that no one misses the grace of God and that no bitter root grows up to cause trouble and defile many" (Heb. 12:15). A bitter person tends to spread the poison in their heart to others around them. Friendships often break up through bitterness, and then mutual friends are forced to choose sides, which leads to more trouble and pain.

Bitterness is a toxic root that grows in the garden of your heart if left unchecked. Usually we do not see the root, just the surface problem. Many people spend a lot of time and effort trying to beautify the outside of their lives, pulling up the surface weeds when really they need to go below the surface and dig up the root.

The verse in Hebrews about a root of bitterness starts by saying, "See to it that no one misses the grace of God" (12:15). Another translation talks about *"pulling back"* from the grace of God. Bitterness does exactly this. It causes a person to pull back from the grace of God.

The first time I was arrested for the gospel in China was very difficult. Somehow in my heart I thought that as a servant of God I was entitled to special treatment in prison. I did receive special treatment, but not the kind I was hoping for! I was severely beaten until my whole body was covered in blood and bruises, and much of my hair was torn from my scalp.

For a time I harbored bitterness against the men who had done this to me, but the gracious Lord Jesus taught me that there is absolutely no point in withholding forgiveness towards anyone, regardless of what they have done. Unforgiveness would only achieve two things. First, it would harden my heart and cause a root of bitterness to take hold, and second, my relationship with Jesus Christ would be damaged. I came to realize that self-righteousness had risen up in my heart. In effect, I was saying to God, "Everybody else should get what they deserve, but don't we have a special relationship, with grace for me?"

It doesn't work like that.

Jesus taught, "Blessed are the merciful, for they will be shown mercy" (Matt. 5:7). God wants us to forgive others of their offences as He has forgiven us of our sins and offences. In fact, Jesus ties *our* forgiveness to whether or not we are willing to forgive others. He said, "For if you forgive men when they sin against you, your heavenly Father will also forgive you. But if you do not forgive men their sins, your Father will not forgive your sins" (Matt. 6:14–15).

There is only one way to dig out the stubborn root of bitterness from our hearts.

It is to forgive.

Too many of God's children have lost their way and live in spiritual captivity because of unforgiveness. They can't hear God's voice, and their lives lack direction and joy.

How are we to forgive others? The apostle Paul told us, "Be kind and compassionate to one another, forgiving each other, just as in Christ God forgave you" (Eph. 4:32), and "Bear with each other and forgive whatever grievances you may have against one another. Forgive as the Lord forgave you" (Col. 3:13).

We are to forgive others the same way that the Lord Jesus forgave us. How did He forgive us?

Unconditionally.

Freely.

Generously.

And without keeping a record of past wrongs.

Don't think that the person who has wronged you must first ask for forgiveness before you can give it. This is a dangerous way of thinking. Even at the very moment that the angry crowd were baying for His blood, Jesus prayed, "Father, forgive them, for they do not know what they are doing" (Luke 23:34).

I know many disciples in China who have spent decades of their lives in prison for the sake of the gospel. Despite unmentionable cruelties being done to them, these men and women are free! Long ago they forgave their persecutors, even though the prison guards and police officers never came to them and asked. Dear friend, even if somebody has committed the most heinous sin against you and has never admitted it or shown the slightest inclination to do so, you still must forgive them. If you can forgive them from your heart, you will be free, and the prison doors that have kept you confined will be opened.

Reconciliation requires two parties to come together and sort out their differences. Forgiveness requires only one. We forgive not to set the other person free, but to set ourselves free. If that person wants to be free, they will have to go to the Lord. We don't have to carry the burden of bitterness anymore!

Forgiveness does not mean that people who have committed heinous crimes will get away with it. Not at all. Rather, forgiveness is the act of releasing our own desire for vengeance and leaving it in God's hands. Listen to what the Bible says:

> *If it is possible, as far as it depends on you, live at peace with everyone. Do not take revenge, my friends, but leave room for God's wrath, for it is written: "It is mine to avenge; I will repay," says the Lord. On the contrary: "If your enemy is hungry, feed him; if he is thirsty, give him something to drink. In doing this, you will heap burning coals on his head."*
>
> *Romans 12:18–20*

The gospel is about restoring our relationship to God, and

also about restoring our relationships with other people. When we fail to show this in our lives, our witness is rendered powerless. In effect, our mouths would be claiming that God can forgive our sins, but our actions would be showing that we are unwilling to extend that forgiveness to others.

Jesus taught:

> *"If you love those who love you, what credit is that to you? Even 'sinners' love those who love them. And if you do good to those who are good to you, what credit is that to you? Even 'sinners' do that.... But love your enemies, do good to them, and lend to them without expecting to get anything back. Then your reward will be great, and you will be sons of the Most High, because he is kind to the ungrateful and wicked. Be merciful, just as your Father is merciful."*
>
> Luke 6:32–33, 35–36

You may be reading this book and thinking, "You don't understand. I have a *right* to feel the way I do. All this forgiveness talk is easy, but I have tried it and it didn't change me much." Other people have told me, "You can't ask people who have been through the most horrific situations to forgive those who did these acts against them! You can't put this extra burden on the victims."

People who think like this have never understood what forgiveness is all about.

Forgiveness is not a burden. It is an offer.

I have also had some difficult experiences in my life. I have had sharp metal needles jabbed under my fingernails until I passed out from the pain. My legs have been smashed by prison guards. On one occasion my body was so destroyed that when my family members came to the prison, they did not recognize me. They told the guards they had brought out the wrong man, and only when my mother noticed my birthmark did they realize it was me. I have been lied about and denounced by other Christian leaders so many times, I can't recall. Yet by the grace of God, I have freely forgiven all of those who brought pain into my life.

Joseph was another man who could easily have become bitter. Did you ever think about what he faced? As a seventeen-year-old boy, Joseph was betrayed by his brothers and sold into slavery in a foreign land. In Egypt he was falsely accused of attempted rape and spent years rotting in prison for a crime he didn't commit.

All of this happened to Joseph *after* God had given him a vision.

I'm sure Joseph struggled with bitterness. I'm sure he often thought, "How could my brothers do this to me?" There were countless ways that Joseph could have justified any bitterness he felt in his heart, but he didn't. Faced with all these temptations, Joseph was able to realize that he belonged first and foremost to God, and he chose to live according to the laws and principles of His kingdom.

During those years of struggle, God was forming a message in Joseph. Joseph was learning about forgiveness. Later, he would not just be able to speak about forgiveness; he would be a living testimony to it.

You may have heard a hundred sermons on forgiveness before, but the only way those messages will become a reality in your life is if you receive an opportunity to forgive someone.

Joseph had a choice. Either he could become bitter and hardened by his experiences, or he could become like soft clay in the hands of the Potter. He chose the latter. We know that Joseph did not become bitter, because he was well liked in the prison. Bitter people are never well liked.

God eventually turned Joseph's situation around, and he was miraculously promoted from the prison to the second in command in all of Egypt. The Bible says that "Joseph was thirty years old when he entered the service of Pharaoh king of Egypt" (Gen. 41:46). It had been thirteen long years since Joseph's brothers had mistreated him.

We cannot find a trace of bitterness when Joseph finally came face-to-face with his brothers. He could easily have used his new powerful position to get revenge, but we read of nothing but love for those who had wronged him. Joseph's brothers were afraid and on one occasion even asked, "What if Joseph holds a grudge against us and pays us back for all the wrongs we did to him?" (50:15). They need not have worried, for such was the change God had brought about in Joseph's character that he struggled to hold back the tears of joy when his brothers stood before him.

Joseph had become a broken man with a deep trust in God. He was able to tell his family, "'Don't be afraid.... You intended to harm me, but God intended it for good to accomplish what is now being done, the saving of many lives. So then, don't be afraid. I will provide for you and your children.' And he reassured them and spoke kindly to them" (50:19–21).

Whatever painful experiences you have had in your life, I encourage you also to freely forgive, because Jesus has forgiven all of your sins and offences.

Jesus invites you to walk with Him on the path of forgiveness – the path of freedom. Forgiveness is a great gift that God has given us so we can survive in an evil world where people hurt us, betray us and do terrible things to us. When we have learned to live in a flow of forgiveness, we will be living in freedom.

Dear friend, I encourage you to put this book down and spend some time in prayer, asking the Holy Spirit to show you if there is anyone you hold unforgiveness towards in your heart. You might consider getting a pen and piece of paper and writing down the names of those who have wronged you in the past, whom you have yet to fully release to the Lord.

Then ask God to forgive them by name, and ask Him to help you release those people into His hands and to set you free. A heart of bitterness and unforgiveness is like a prison. It not only binds others, but it also destroys you. Jesus is the great gardener, and He is able to uproot even the deepest root of bitterness in your heart.

I exhort you in the name of Jesus Christ to get rid of all bitterness and learn to forgive, before the bitterness develops a deep root that is difficult to weed out of your life. The Bible says, "If you harbor bitter envy and selfish ambition in your hearts, do not boast about it or deny the truth. Such 'wisdom' does not come down from heaven but is earthly, unspiritual, of the devil. For where you have envy and selfish ambition, there you find disorder and every evil practice" (James 3:14–16).

Praise the Lord! He can set you free.

Jesus wants your life to have living water flowing from it, bringing blessing and refreshment to others around you. Forgiveness is an essential step in the process of becoming a vessel of blessing. As you head into the future with your past wiped clean, ask Jesus to teach you how to walk in forgiveness, so that future offences will be quickly put aside and handed to God.

Then you will truly be free!

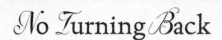

No Turning Back

Could we with ink the ocean fill,
And were the skies of parchment made,
Were every stalk on earth a quill,
And every man a scribe by trade,
To write the love of God above
Would drain the ocean dry;
Nor could the scroll contain the whole,
Tho stretched from sky to sky.

*Words found scratched on the wall of an insane
asylum in California, 1917*

We love because he first loved us.

1 John 4:19

The greatest plan of God on this earth is His plan of salvation. We need to realize that salvation originates from God and not from us. The Bible says that we love God because He first loved us, and Jesus plainly told His followers, "You did not choose me, but I chose you and appointed you to go and bear fruit—fruit that will last" (John 15:16).

Jesus loves you and has called you to follow Him. He shares

His visions and plans with all of His children who are willing to quiet their hearts and listen. Realizing that the power to serve Jesus comes from God will give us unwavering faith and boldness: "So we say with confidence, 'The Lord is my helper; I will not be afraid. What can man do to me?'" (Heb. 13:6).

I pray that these messages will help equip you to serve the Lord Jesus Christ wholeheartedly, so that your life will bring glory to the King of Kings and result in many lost souls coming into the kingdom of God.

When God reveals His plans and strategies to us, we must move forward in obedience and be willing to withstand attacks and opposition. We need to recognize that just because a heavenly calling has come to our lives, it doesn't mean everything will go smoothly. In fact, it could be argued that Satan only attacks those plans that he knows originate from God's throne. Other kinds of plans and programs that Christians are involved with are little threat to Satan's kingdom on this earth. But when our adversary senses something has God's anointing on it, he is afraid, for such strategies can blow his evil kingdom to pieces.

The disciples of Jesus received a calling from God to take the gospel to the ends of the earth. They went forth in obedience and in the power of God, and they paid a dear price for their service. Historians record how the apostles were martyred in the most barbaric manner imaginable. For many years in China, we have sung a powerful song called "Martyrs for the Lord." The lyrics recall what happened to the early followers of Jesus and exhort us to follow in their footsteps:

> *From the time the church was birthed on the day of*
> *Pentecost*
> *The followers of the Lord have willingly sacrificed*
> *themselves*

*Tens of thousands have died that the gospel might
    prosper*
As such they have obtained the crown of life

Chorus:
*To be a martyr for the Lord, to be a martyr for the
    Lord*
I am willing to die gloriously for the Lord

Those apostles who loved the Lord to the end
*Willingly followed the Lord down the path of
    suffering*
John was exiled to the lonely isle of Patmos
Stephen was stoned to death by an angry crowd
Matthew was stabbed to death in Persia by a mob
Mark died as horses pulled his two legs apart
Doctor Luke was cruelly hanged
Peter, Philip and Simon were crucified on a cross
Bartholomew was skinned alive by the heathen
*Thomas died in India as five horses pulled his body
    apart*
The apostle James was beheaded by King Herod
Little James was cut in half by a sharp saw
James the brother of the Lord was stoned to death
Judas was tied to a pillar and shot by arrows
Matthias had his head cut off in Jerusalem
Paul was a martyr under Emperor Nero
I am willing to take up the cross and go forward
To follow the apostles down the road of sacrifice
That tens of thousands of precious souls can be saved
*I am willing to leave all and be a martyr for the
    Lord.*

In the twenty centuries since the New Testament was written, many millions of Christ's followers have been slaughtered around the world, thus gaining a martyr's crown. These were men and women, boys and girls who loved the Lord Jesus and had received a heavenly calling. And yet on the path of obeying that calling, they were required to shed their blood and die for the God who first died for them.

In this context, you should not be surprised when the vision you have received encounters such severe opposition, nor should you be surprised when hardship and persecution become your close companions as you walk on the road of obedience to God.

The covenant between the Lord and His followers is based on the spilling of blood. It is a most serious covenant. Jesus told His disciples, "This cup is the new covenant in my blood, which is poured out for you" (Luke 22:20). Jesus made the ultimate commitment to us. He willingly gave His life to be slaughtered like a defenseless lamb, so that He would become "the head of the body, the church ... the beginning and the firstborn from among the dead, so that in everything he might have the supremacy" (Col. 1:18).

Jesus' commitment to die for us is a foundational truth. For this reason, whenever you partake in the Lord's Supper, you must do so with a reverent and humble attitude. It is a serious privilege, and all who treat the Lord's Supper disrespectfully, without giving due attention to its meaning, are on dangerous ground, for they are disrespecting the sacrifice of Jesus Christ. That is why the Bible says, "For anyone who eats and drinks without recognizing the body of the Lord eats and drinks judgment on himself. That is why many among you are weak and sick, and a number of you have fallen asleep. But if we judged ourselves, we would not come under judgment" (1 Cor. 11:29–31).

The covenant between Jesus and His followers is based on the shedding of blood and sacrifice. But what about us? Should we expect to minister for Jesus in relative peace and calm, or are we required to make the same commitment that Jesus made for us? The Bible is very clear:

> *To this you were called, because Christ suffered for you, leaving you an example, that you should follow in his steps.*
>
> *1 Peter 2:21*

> *Remember the words I spoke to you: "No servant is greater than his master." If they persecuted me, they will persecute you also. If they obeyed my teaching, they will obey yours also. They will treat you this way because of my name, for they do not know the One who sent me.*
>
> *John 15:20–21*

You see, we are not only called to follow a suffering Master. We are also called to suffer for His kingdom and to endure to the end. If you have a calling from God, it will take courage, faith and endurance to see it become a reality. Paul encouraged Timothy, "Endure hardship with us like a good soldier of Christ Jesus" (2 Tim. 2:3).

Please don't fall into a trap of thinking that persecution and hardship are things that only Christians on the other side of the world from where you live will experience. No! These are promised to every follower of Christ, irrespective of their country, culture or government. "In fact, everyone who wants to live a godly life in Christ Jesus will be persecuted, while evil men and impostors will go from bad to worse, deceiving and being deceived" (2 Tim. 3:12–13).

Do you want to follow God and do something great for His kingdom?

If so, then good.

But you must first realize that the pathway to bearing fruit for the Lord is strewn with much opposition, slander, criticism, false accusation and pain. People will misunderstand you and doubt your motives, and Satan will throw many roadblocks in your path in a bid to thwart your progress. This has been my experience over the years, and it has been the experience of every person I have known who has been used by God, from the apostles to the present day.

The good news is that our Lord provides comfort and grace to all of His children as they follow the vision He has given them. He does not abandon us to our own devices; otherwise none of us would survive. His love has sustained me in my darkest times, and His comfort has overwhelmed me when I have been in prison for the Lord for the sake of the gospel. Whatever Satan and evil men might throw at you, the love of God more than compensates. The apostle Paul knew this when he wrote the following powerful verses:

> Who shall separate us from the love of Christ? Shall trouble or hardship or persecution or famine or nakedness or danger or sword? As it is written: "For your sake we face death all day long; we are considered as sheep to be slaughtered." No, in all these things we are more than conquerors through him who loved us. For I am convinced that neither death nor life, neither angels nor demons, neither the present nor the future, nor any powers, neither height nor depth, nor anything else in

*all creation, will be able to separate us from the love of God
that is in Christ Jesus our Lord.*

Romans 8:35–39

As you step out in obedience to a heavenly vision, be encouraged! God will help you so that it comes to pass. But gird yourself for a battle against the forces of darkness. You must determine in your heart not to give up, for "we are not of those who shrink back and are destroyed, but of those who believe and are saved" (Heb. 10:39).

5

The Pregnancy of the Holy Spirit

Where there is no vision, the people perish.

Proverbs 29:18 KJV

In the gospel of Luke we find the remarkable account of how Mary became pregnant by the Holy Spirit and gave birth to the Son of God, the Savior of the world.

God, in His matchless wisdom, safely brought the birth of His Son to fruition, but the Devil was not finished with his plan to wipe out Jesus. He attempted to destroy the newborn King by motivating Herod to slaughter all of the boys under the age of two in Bethlehem. Once again, God in His infinite power protected His Son, who was carried away to safety in Egypt before the carnage commenced.

During this intense time, with Satan throwing all of his energy toward obliterating the Anointed One from the face of the earth, God not only prevented this from occurring, but even orchestrated events so that His beloved Son received worship from a variety of people, including a group of shepherds working near Bethlehem at the time of the birth. At the other end of the social scale, a number of princely men – known as magi – traveled from faraway Gentile nations in order to bow down and pay homage to the Prince of Peace.

It is interesting that God chose such a collection of people to be the first to worship Jesus. Historians tell us that shepherds at the time were considered the scum of society. They were considered to be compulsive liars and thieves and of such poor character that they were not even allowed to testify in court. It reveals much of the nature, love and grace of God that He chose a group of shepherds to be the first to hear of the Messiah's birth.

The magi, on the other hand, were probably the greatest scholars and scientists in the world at the time. They were skilled astronomers and had spent years studying and recording the celestial bodies. In China, many Christians believe one of the magi who went to worship Jesus came from our land. At the time, the Silk Road was already functioning between China and Israel, and there is anecdotal evidence that the leading astronomer in the emperor's court left China for two years at around the time of the birth of Christ in order to follow what the ancients called the "King Star." There are similar accounts of magi from Babylon (today's Iraq), Persia (Iran) and other parts of Central Asia and the Middle East.

By bringing these diverse groups of people to see Jesus, God revealed that the good news would be for all people everywhere. Even those outcasts considered the scum of society (shepherds) would not be excluded from salvation in God's kingdom, nor would the wealthy and highly educated magi from Gentile nations.

The first that Mary knew anything about God's plan

was when the archangel Gabriel visited the Virgin Mary and announced:

> *"Greetings, you who are highly favored! The Lord is with you. . . . You will be with child and give birth to a son, and you are to give him the name Jesus. He will be great and will be called the Son of the Most High. The Lord God will give him the throne of his father David, and he will reign over the house of Jacob forever; his kingdom will never end."*

> *Luke 1:28, 31–33*

Can you imagine how shocked Mary must have been? Not surprisingly, she asked the angel how this could happen, as she had not been with any man. Gabriel answered, "The Holy Spirit will come upon you, and the power of the Most High will overshadow you. So the holy one to be born will be called the Son of God. Even Elizabeth your relative is going to have a child in her old age, and she who was said to be barren is in her sixth month. For nothing is impossible with God" (Luke 1:35–37).

Mary became pregnant, and in due time she gave birth to the Son of God.

Do you realize that God wants all Christians to be pregnant with the Holy Spirit today? He wants to give you a vision for His kingdom that originates from heaven, not from yourself. He desires that all of His children would be overshadowed by His presence in such a way that they are changed and give birth to something in their lives that brings many into His kingdom.

Now is the time that the Holy Spirit is moving powerfully among us. The message I want to share is that you must be willing to become pregnant by the Holy Spirit. When a heavenly vision comes to dwell inside of your innermost being, the whole direction of your life will be changed.

It is clear that God chose to honor Mary because He knew she would be willing and obedient to His heavenly plan. Mary's humble and submissive character is seen in her reply to Gabriel: "I am the Lord's servant. May it be to me as you have said" (Luke 1:38).

It doesn't matter what your situation is today – whether you are young or old, married or single, wealthy or poor – God wants you to be obedient and submissive to the Holy Spirit so that He can create new life in you that will bless the world. Elizabeth also experienced a miraculous pregnancy, even though she was barren and "well along in years" (Luke 1:7). If you are willing to receive the Holy Spirit into your life, I am confident you will see mighty things from our great God, even if you feel old and your Christian life seems dry and barren.

I am sure that God wants to indwell and empower you because I have seen this occur in my own life, and I have seen it happen throughout my nation. In the last few decades, as many as 100,000,000 people in China have started to follow Jesus Christ. The good news has been carried into all corners of China by men and women who were willing to become pregnant by the Holy Spirit.

After the Revolution in 1949, the Christians in my country were persecuted. Churches were destroyed or turned into gymnasiums, granaries or government offices. All of the foreign missionaries were expelled and sent back to their home countries. The spirit of atheism swept like a forest fire throughout China until it had scarred the whole land. Thousands of pastors and church leaders were executed or thrown into prison for many years. Hundreds spent more than two decades performing hard labor in dire prison camps for no other reason except that they loved Jesus Christ. Many died from sheer exhaustion or from starvation. To anyone on the outside looking in, it appeared there was no church left in China. It seemed to have been totally obliterated.

Then in the 1970s, God started to do something. At first, just a little seed appeared, and some tiny pockets of believers reappeared above the surface after decades in hiding. These small seeds started to take root, and in due time, a little stem poked its way above the ground. After enjoying the warmth of the sun's rays and being watered by the expert Gardener, the stem sprouted branches, growing taller and stronger with each passing day. By the early 1980s, thousands of trees had emerged throughout China, and they, in turn, produced many seeds that were blown far and wide by the wind of the Holy Spirit. Thousands of believers turned into millions as revival swept our nation, and millions turned into tens of millions, and now even 100,000,000!

This great revival happened after God found people who were willing to be pregnant by the Holy Spirit. They were available and willing to preach the gospel to every part of China. I was just one among a multitude who bowed down and committed my life to serve Jesus and to take His message wherever the Lord told us to go, irrespective of what hardships came our way. Plenty of hard times did come my way, but the Lord sustained me throughout it all.

It seems that when the Lord first speaks to people, often their initial reaction is to be afraid. Elizabeth's husband, Zechariah, did not receive the news of her impending pregnancy positively and was silenced until after the birth (see Luke

1:19–20). Many Christians are likewise afraid of the Word of the Lord when it first comes to them.

Dear friend, I encourage you not to be afraid of hearing God's voice and obeying Him! God can never lie, nor can He ever abandon His children. He can be trusted completely. Step out in faith and confidence, knowing that "he who began a good work in you will carry it on to completion until the day of Christ Jesus" (Phil. 1:6).

Today much Christian activity seems to originate with human plans, and it is then carried out in human strength, with human results. It has nothing to do with the kingdom of God. The world does not need any more religion! It needs Jesus Christ. Religion is people's attempts to do God's work in their own strength. Jesus wants us to live and walk in God's strength.

God is only interested in His work, not our work. He oversees and empowers those things that originate in His heart. On judgment day, only that which was birthed and sustained by the Holy Spirit will survive. Paul told the church in Corinth:

> *If any man builds on this foundation using gold, silver, costly stones, wood, hay or straw, his work will be shown for what it is, because the Day will bring it to light. It will be revealed with fire, and the fire will test the quality of each man's work. If what he has built survives, he will receive his reward. If it is burned up, he will suffer loss; he himself will be saved, but only as one escaping through the flames.*
>
> *1 Corinthians 3:12–15*

Trying to live the Christian life in your own strength and by your own efforts is a very frustrating and futile experience.

We need to ask God to humble us and to make us realize He is in charge. Our role is simply to hear His voice, to give our lives unreservedly so that we may become pregnant by the Holy Spirit and to obey His command to reach this sick and hurting world.

When Mary said, "May it be to me as you have said," do you think she expected her submission to God's will would be easy? I don't think so. She knew that becoming pregnant outside of marriage would result in being misunderstood and rejected by society. Mary was undoubtedly aware that she might be accused of adultery and stoned to death, as the Jewish law demanded. She knew people would mock and despise her.

If you become pregnant by the Holy Spirit, it's very important that you go and visit someone else who is also pregnant by the Holy Spirit. Only people who are also going through this experience can provide encouragement and comfort when others are attacking you. I miss the close fellowship I used to have with such brothers in China. We who were pregnant with the Holy Spirit would often come together for days of prayer and worship, and we would leave greatly strengthened in Christ and able to withstand the dangers and attacks of the world.

Mary sought out Elizabeth, who was also pregnant. Pay careful attention to what happened:

> When Elizabeth heard Mary's greeting, the baby leaped in her womb, and Elizabeth was filled with the Holy Spirit. In a loud voice she exclaimed: "Blessed are you among women, and blessed is the child you will bear! But why am I so favored, that the mother of my Lord should come to me? As soon as the sound of your greeting reached my ears, the baby

in my womb leaped for joy. Blessed is she who has believed
that what the Lord has said to her will be accomplished!"

Luke 1:41–45

When you become pregnant with a vision from the Holy Spirit, seek out your Elizabeth. Such a person will not mock or condemn you for obeying God's call on your life. Unfortunately, there are many in the church today who will do all they can to stamp out your call and enthusiasm for the Lord. Spend as much time as you can with others who are pregnant by the Holy Spirit. I know that each time you see them, something will jump inside your spirit!

If you are willing to become pregnant by the Holy Spirit, don't be afraid! God will sustain you and complete the birth of that which is inside of you. At the same time, you should realize that giving birth is often a painful experience. For the joy of being pregnant by the Holy Spirit, I have been called to endure persecution and torture for the sake of the gospel. I have been blessed to be sent to various prisons so that I could preach the gospel to those who needed to drink the living water of Jesus Christ. All of this was worth it for the great joy of seeing God glorified as He blessed and saved people through that which He placed inside of me. Jesus taught, "A woman giving birth to a child has pain because her time has come; but when her baby is born she forgets the anguish because of her joy that a child is born into the world" (John 16:21).

Our loving heavenly Father is looking for people who are willing to become pregnant with His presence, vision and power. Don't make any more excuses. Don't say you are too young or too old, for God wants to work in you and through you in a mighty way.

Are you willing to surrender control of your life into the hands of God?

Will you be like Mary and pray, "I am the Lord's servant; may it be to me as you have said"?

You will never regret such a prayer.

6

The Person God Uses

> At that time Jesus, full of joy through the Holy Spirit, said, "I praise you, Father, Lord of heaven and earth, because you have hidden these things from the wise and learned, and revealed them to little children. Yes, Father, for this was your good pleasure."
>
> *Luke 10:21*

Since leaving China I have come to see there is a serious misunderstanding among many Christians around the world when it comes to being a worker in God's kingdom. In the West, especially, the gospel has been intellectualized to such an extent that there is almost no mention of true faith and trust in Jesus anymore. Academic qualifications and speaking ability are held in high regard, while spiritual maturity, character and the call of the Holy Spirit have been relegated in importance and largely consigned to being irrelevant when it comes to God's work.

Of course this is nonsense and completely against the teachings of the Bible. If men can do God's work in their own strength, then it is not God's work at all. The Lord Jesus calls people who realize they cannot function at all apart from His grace and empowerment. Such an attitude results in complete dependence on God, and this is good in His sight. If we can accomplish tasks without God, then He will not get the glory. People will look at what we have done and give us the credit. But if we do something that is completely impossible apart from God's supernatural intervention, people have no choice but to give glory to God.

As I have shared about the Back to Jerusalem vision of the Chinese church, some Western Christians have said we will not be able to successfully impact the Muslim, Buddhist and Hindu nations with the gospel unless we first gain more qualifications and training. Some Christian journalists have even gone so far as to mock our plans, claiming that people from poor, uneducated farming backgrounds will never be able to serve God, and that only Christians with university degrees have a chance at fruitful ministry.

Is this true?

What do the Scriptures say? What kind of person does God use in His kingdom? Are the house church believers in China wasting their time? Would we do better to forget about cross-cultural missionary work? It soon becomes apparent that the weight of Scripture, Christian history and modern experience does not support such thinking.

Far from selecting the most qualified for the task of missionaries, Jesus specifically chose young men from farming and fishing backgrounds to be among his twelve disciples. Simon and his brother Andrew were busy casting their nets into the lake when Jesus called them to follow. These two fishermen were the very first disciples Jesus chose. James and John were the next two called as disciples (see Matt. 4:18–22). They too were fishermen. When Jesus found them, they were in their father's boat preparing to cast their nets.

Certainly there were professionals in his team as well, even Matthew the tax collector, but most were simple rural men who knew how to work with their hands. They were rough—especially the strong-willed Simon Peter—but Jesus looked past the rough exterior and saw a polished diamond inside.

These men formed the leadership of the first missionary era and turned their generation upside down. The apostle Paul, himself a tent maker, had a team of disciples with him at various times on his travels. His companions included the doctor Luke (Col. 4:14) and Zenas, who was a lawyer (Titus 3:13), but there was also room for less sophisticated people, even for Onesimus the slave (Philem. 10).

All throughout history, the church of Jesus Christ has grown through the consecrated lives of committed men and women, irrespective of their social, economic or educational background. Peasants have testified before kings, and farmers have been used mightily by God to shake whole nations. God even once chose a shepherd boy to be king of Israel!

The way of the world is always to look at human credentials as the prerequisite for success. We look for the strongest, most attractive, most educated, thinking that God's work can be accomplished through human effort.

God, however, clearly uses a different set of scales when he weighs a person. He looks at the character and heart of each individual. Even the great prophet Samuel used worldly thinking when he saw Eliab. The Bible records, "Samuel saw Eliab and thought, 'Surely the LORD's anointed stands here before the LORD.' But the LORD said to Samuel, 'Do not consider his appearance or his height, for I have rejected him. The LORD does not look at the things man looks at. Man looks at the outward appearance, but the LORD looks at the heart'" (1 Sam. 16:6–7).

A university degree has never been a prerequisite for missionary activity. Certainly secular qualifications may help a Christian who has been led by the Holy Spirit to obtain them, but what counts most is a call from God and a heart of passion for the Lord Jesus.

Let's consider the apostle Paul. Before his dramatic conversion to Jesus, Paul had received a very high education. After he was arrested in Jerusalem, he told the angry mob, "I am a Jew, born in Tarsus of Cilicia, but brought up in this city. Under Gamaliel I was thoroughly trained in the law of our fathers and was just as zealous for God as any of you are today" (Acts 22:3).

If anyone had the right to boast about his worldly qualifications, it was the apostle Paul. He told the Philippians, "If anyone else thinks he has reasons to put confidence in the flesh, I have more: circumcised on the eighth day, of the people of Israel, of the tribe of Benjamin, a Hebrew of Hebrews; in regard to the law, a Pharisee; as for zeal, persecuting the church; as for legalistic righteousness, faultless" (Phil. 3:4–6).

Then Paul met the Lord Jesus Christ, and everything changed.

This well-educated and zealous man was humbled under the hand of the almighty God, and he experienced a radical shift in his perspective. Paul told the Philippians, "Whatever was to my profit I now consider loss for the sake of Christ. What is more, I consider everything a loss compared to the surpassing greatness of knowing Christ Jesus my Lord, for whose sake I have lost all things. I consider them rubbish, that I may gain Christ and be found in him, not having a righteousness of my own that comes from the law, but that which is through faith in Christ – the righteousness that comes from God and is by faith" (Phil. 3:7–9).

This man who had once been so full of his own achievements and arrogance that he boldly persecuted the followers of God now counted his life prior to knowing Christ as a pile of rubbish. He had found the truth, and the truth had set him free! As a young man Paul had brought suffering to Christians, but now he was willing to suffer himself for the sake of Christ. He concluded, "I want to know Christ and the power of his resurrection and the fellowship of sharing in his sufferings, becoming like him in his death, and so, somehow, to attain to the resurrection from the dead" (Phil. 3:10–11).

How about you? Do you also realize that all human achievement apart from God is rubbish? Or do you think the Lord only wants to use people with secular qualifications and eloquent personalities?

God never calls anyone to serve Him in their own strength, knowledge or qualifications. He calls people to serve Him through relationship with the Father, humility and obedience. Our Lord requires that instead of being full of ourselves, we empty ourselves on His altar and become like John the Baptist, who declared, "He must become greater; I must become less" (John 3:30).

God can certainly use educated people. I'm not saying we all have to be stupid to serve Him! But what I am saying is that if all we have is our human wisdom, we will not be able to produce any fruit for the kingdom of God. The apostle Paul did not rely on his own wisdom and knowledge to serve God. Indeed, listen to what he told the Corinthians: "When I came to you, brothers, I did not come with eloquence or superior wisdom as I proclaimed to you the testimony about God. For I resolved to know nothing while I was with you except Jesus Christ and him crucified. I came to you in weakness and fear, and with much trembling" (1 Cor. 2:1–3).

Brothers and sisters, let me tell you something crucial: God chooses to use those individuals who know Him intimately! This is the primary qualification for service in the kingdom of God. "The people who know their God shall be strong, and carry out great exploits" (Dan. 11:32 NKJV).

There is so much Christian activity being done in the name of the Lord today that does not have His power or presence at its core. Countless sermons are preached every week in churches around the world that are full of man's wisdom but totally devoid of the power and presence of the Holy Spirit. Such "work" is tragic and never produces true fruit for the kingdom of God.

Friends, do not be deceived into thinking you need more human qualifications and degrees before you can serve God! This is the opposite of what the Bible says. It is better to commit yourself afresh to Him and ask the Lord to use you for His glory. Such a willing and obedient servant thrills the heart of God. The Bible clearly states the qualifications for serving God:

> *He has showed you, O man, what is good.*
> *And what does the LORD require of you?*
> *To act justly and to love mercy*
> *and to walk humbly with your God.*
>
> *Micah 6:8*

When Peter and John were hauled before the Sanhedrin, the religious leaders could not understand how the two fishermen could speak with such authority and clarity. "When they saw the courage of Peter and John and realized that they were unschooled, ordinary men, they were astonished and they took note that these men had been with Jesus" (Acts 4:13).

Those among us who are "unschooled and ordinary" need not be discouraged. God has not despised the simple farmers and laborers throughout history, and He continues to use them today!

Recently I was invited to a mission conference. The delegates came from churches and organizations in twenty-six countries. During the conference I was asked, "Do you think Communism in China will collapse and the nation splinter, like what happened in the former Soviet Union?" I answered, "Many Christian leaders may have different opinions on this matter. I don't know what political changes will happen to my country, but I do know that God called me to preach the gospel to the South, to the West and to the unreached nations between China and Jerusalem. I have no idea if the political system in China will collapse, but what I do know is that China needs Jesus Christ, and Muslim and Buddhist nations need Jesus Christ."

You see, I believe Jesus Christ alone is the answer for the ills of the whole world. Communism is not the answer, but neither is democracy. It is God's will that must rule, and His kingdom that must reign on earth as it is heaven. Democracy may be good in many ways, but it is a concept not supported in Scripture. If democracy was the rule of law in God's kingdom, then Moses would never have led Israel out of Egypt, for the majority of Israelites grumbled against Moses and even wanted him put to death. If they had listened to the voice of democracy, Caleb and Joshua would have been overruled, for those two men went against the advice of all the other spies who returned from the Promised Land. When God commanded me to stand up and walk out of prison in 1997, there was no need to hold a meeting to discuss it with the other believers. When the Almighty speaks, all other voices fall silent.

Moses overcame many obstacles because he was faithful to obey the vision God gave him. Similarly, Joshua and Caleb would not allow the fear of man to get in the way of their God-given vision. The person whom God uses is the one who receives a vision from God and is then faithful to step out and obey what He has revealed to them. On the other hand, if we run our lives by trying to secure approval from others before we act, we will not progress very far. The cowardly Pilate gave in to the voice of the multitudes and sentenced Jesus to be crucified.

Jesus alone is the head of the church and the source of all life. All nations must follow Him. Governments and politicians might set their own agendas, but vision comes from God alone. He is in charge of the whole world. The arrogant King Nebuchadnezzar was so proud that it took seven years of being humbled by God before he was finally able to declare, "The Most High is sovereign over the kingdoms of men and gives them to anyone he wishes" (Dan. 4:32).

As followers of Jesus Christ, we should pray for a revelation of God's sovereign power over the affairs of humankind. God is always on the throne, and nothing takes Him by surprise! When such a realization seeps down into our spirits, we will no longer be fearful of the future or worried about the storms that rage around us. Like the infant Moses who was safe in the waterproof basket his mother lovingly made for him, you will be secure in God's protective love as you travel through this world as "aliens and strangers on earth" (Heb. 11:13). Such people are "looking forward to the city with foundations, whose architect and builder is God" (Heb. 11:10).

If you want to be a person whom God uses, it is vital for you to have a deep revelation of God's sovereignty and authority. When you gain such an understanding, you will have bold faith and will be able to face the enemy knowing that your God is stronger than all. When you face the enemy, however, you must not trust in your own power and wisdom, or you will be doomed to failure. Christians are not called to understand everything as we serve God. We are simply called to obey and step out in faith.

Let us carefully consider the words of the apostle Paul: "Where is the wise man? Where is the scholar? Where is the philosopher of this age? Has not God made foolish the wisdom of the world? For since in the wisdom of God the world through its wisdom did not know him, God was pleased through the foolishness of what was preached to save those who believe ... For the foolishness of God is wiser than man's wisdom, and the weakness of God is stronger than man's strength.

Brothers, think of what you were when you were called. Not many of you were wise by human standards; not many were influential; not many were of noble birth. But God chose the foolish things of the world to shame the wise; God chose the weak things of the world to shame the strong. He chose the lowly things of this world and the despised things – and the things that are not – to nullify the things that are, so that no one may boast before him" (1 Cor. 1:20–21, 25–29).

As you serve the Lord and He begins to use you, be careful not to turn your ministry into an idol. Keep your heart soft before the Lord and don't get so busy that you lose perspective. This has happened to me on a few occasions during my life, but the Lord always helped me repent by removing me and giving me a time in prison or in the wilderness.

There are times when God calls us to be alone for a time so that we can get to know Him more intimately. The apostle Paul spent three years in Arabia before starting his ministry (Gal. 1:11–18), and men like Moses, Joseph and Elijah spent years in isolation as God prepared them for the work He had called them to. Even the Lord Jesus Christ spent forty days and nights alone in the wilderness before starting His public ministry. After his ministry commenced, Jesus "often withdrew to lonely places and prayed" (Luke 5:16).

A few years after I left China, all kinds of invitations flooded in for me to speak at meetings and conferences in various parts of the world. At one stage I allowed myself to be scheduled to speak for 120 days in a row, often three or four times per day. In a single month I spoke in 160 meetings! Ministry was becoming an idol, and my inner spiritual life was being neglected. I was feeding God's people with old stale leftovers, as the fresh water of the Holy Spirit was not flowing through my life because I was too busy and exhausted.

It is easy to be deceived when we place ministry in a higher position than it ought to be. Even when I was burned out and giving stale messages, people were still receiving what I had to say and applauding me, even though I was operating outside of the fresh anointing of the Holy Spirit. We can trick ourselves into thinking everything is all right, because the people seem to be blessed by what we have to say.

One day I was boarding an airplane to go to my next series of meetings when the Lord clearly told me, "I hold this against you: You have forsaken your first love. Remember the height from which you have fallen! Repent and do the things you did at first. If you do not repent, I will come to you and remove your lampstand from its place" (Rev. 2:4–5).

The Lord saw that I needed a rest, and He arranged it in a way that only He could. I was arrested in the nation of Myanmar, beaten and sentenced to seven years in prison because of my disobedience to the Holy Spirit. In prison, the Lord showed me that my life was getting out of control and I needed to slow down. This was the second time He allowed me to have a holiday in prison while I learned to renew my relationship with the Lord Jesus.

After I left China, I discovered that pastors in the West have Mondays off and go on summer holidays every year. In China the believers have no opportunity to take holidays, so the Lord graciously becomes our travel agent and books us in for a time of much-needed rest at a prison. I must have had so much vacation time stored up that the Lord allowed me to take all my vacations at once!

These days I put a limit on how often I will travel and speak, so things are much better in my own life and my family is happier too.

It's a wonderful thing when God's children realize we are nothing apart from Him! When we understand that we need to be totally dependent on Him, it takes away all competition, striving and selfish ambition.

May God grant us this understanding every day.

7

Lazarus, Come Out!

> Jesus called in a loud voice, "Lazarus, come out!" The dead man came out, his hands and feet wrapped with strips of linen, and a cloth around his face.
>
> *John 11:43–44*

The love of the Lord Jesus Christ is different from any human love. Even the love a mother has for her children pales in comparison to the incomparable, unchangeable love of God.

People might love you, but one day your life will come to an end and you will be buried in the ground. God loves you so much, however, that death can be just the beginning of an eternity spent in His presence. The apostle John "heard a loud voice from the throne saying, 'Now the dwelling of God is with men, and he will live with them. They will be his people, and God himself will be with them and be their God. He will wipe every tear from their eyes. There will be no more death or mourning or crying or pain, for the old order of things has passed away'" (Rev. 21:3–4).

The power of Jesus is unchangeable. The love and salvation of Jesus are unchangeable. It is we who need to be changed so that we conform to God's character. Such a transformation in our lives is an ongoing process. It starts the moment we begin living for Jesus Christ, but the process of being more like Him will continue until the day we die. "Therefore we do not lose heart. Though outwardly we are wasting away, yet inwardly we are being renewed day by day" (2 Cor. 4:16).

When I preach at churches around the world, I see three different kinds of people present. The first are those people who have a heart like Martha. Martha loved to serve others. She was often busy cooking or doing something that would be a blessing to the Lord and the disciples. Yet Jesus had to rebuke Martha because she had taken her eyes off her relationship with Him and was paying too much attention to serving. This is a danger for everyone who ministers for the Lord.

The second kind of people are those like Martha's sister, Mary. Mary loved to come and sit at Jesus' feet and listen to whatever He had to say. Often those Christians who are busy serving the Lord can be critical of those who spend time just sitting at His feet. Martha started to think Mary wasn't pulling her weight and asked, " 'Lord, don't you care that my sister has left me to do the work by myself? Tell her to help me!' 'Martha, Martha,' the Lord answered, 'you are worried and upset about many things, but only one thing is needed. Mary has chosen what is better, and it will not be taken away from her' " (Luke 10:40–42).

The third kind of people I see in churches around the world are those like Lazarus. He was the brother of Mary and Martha and was a friend of Jesus. When Lazarus died, his sisters "sent word to Jesus, 'Lord, the one you love is sick.' When he heard this, Jesus said, 'This sickness will not end in death. No, it is

for God's glory so that God's Son may be glorified through it'"
(John 11:3–4).

When I came out of China and started speaking in churches
throughout the Western world, I was shocked to discover that
many Christians and churches have very little spiritual warmth
left in them. They may have just a few embers remaining on
the fire of God's altar, but I have good news for you: even those
little embers of coal can reignite when the wind of the Holy
Spirit blows upon you!

When Jesus heard that His friend Lazarus had died, He
told the disciples they would travel back to Judea, where Lazarus lived. The disciples, however, tried to dissuade Jesus from
going. They said:

> "A short while ago the Jews tried to stone you, and yet you
> are going back there?"
>
> Jesus answered, "Are there not twelve hours of daylight?
> A man who walks by day will not stumble, for he sees by this
> world's light. It is when he walks by night that he stumbles,
> for he has no light."
>
> After he had said this, he went on to tell them, "Our
> friend Lazarus has fallen asleep; but I am going there to wake
> him up."
>
> His disciples replied, "Lord, if he sleeps, he will get better."
> Jesus had been speaking of his death, but his disciples thought
> he meant natural sleep.
>
> So then he told them plainly, "Lazarus is dead, and for
> your sake I am glad I was not there, so that you may believe.
> But let us go to him."

John 11:8–15

When Jesus sets His mind to do something, no power in the universe can hinder His plan! When He and the disciples reached Judea, Martha came running out to see Jesus and told Him, "Lord, if you had been here, my brother would not have died" (John 11:21).

I believe the Western church is generally in the same condition as Martha. You know the truths about God's Word in your head, but you still like to run your own lives. Like Martha, many Christians cry out, "Lord, if you had just done things according to our plans, we would never have ended up in such a mess."

Friend, you need to realize that God is not at all interested in *your* plans. He is only interested in *His* plans! So many churches and individual believers think they should make their own plans and strategies, then ask (or in some cases, command) God to bless them.

The almighty God is not our servant! He does not do what we tell Him to do. Many Christians need to climb down from the throne they have built for themselves, fall on their faces before God and do whatever the Master tells them to do.

When Jesus informed Martha that He had come to raise Lazarus from the dead, Martha resorted to her theological knowledge by saying, "I know he will rise again in the resurrection at the last day" (John 11:24). This is a chief attribute of Christians who only know Jesus from a theological viewpoint. They know about the history of God's workings with humankind, and they know that in the future God will make everything right. But they do not know Jesus in the here and now. Jesus has become a historical and future figure, but not a present figure in their daily lives.

Many churches are spiritually dead today because they keep

Jesus at a "safe distance" while they control their own lives and make their own plans. Until you realize that the living Jesus Christ wants to be the major part of everything you do, you will not see revival. Until He is rightfully enthroned as King of Kings and Lord of Lords, your plans will continue to be frustrated and you will see little true blessing of heaven on your activities.

Mary's reaction was better than that of her sister. When Martha told Mary that Jesus had arrived, "she fell at his feet and said, 'Lord, if you had been here, my brother would not have died'" (John 11:32). Mary was in the right position, at Jesus' feet, but she did not fully comprehend the power of God for today.

Jesus was deeply moved by the tears of Mary and the other mourners, and He wept. Then the Bible records, "The Jews said, 'See how he loved him!' But some of them said, 'Could not he who opened the eyes of the blind man have kept this man from dying?'" (John 11:36–37). Isn't it strange that the world often accuses God of not helping in times of trouble and disaster? When there is an earthquake or a tsunami, lots of people suddenly emerge and blame God for not preventing it. The same people who indulge in blatant sin and mock God through their unbelief all of a sudden feel emboldened to criticize and pass judgment on Him when things go wrong.

Jesus went to the cave where Lazarus was buried and asked the onlookers to roll the stone away. Martha didn't want a scene, so she protested, "But, Lord, by this time there is a bad odor, for he has been there four days" (John 11:39). If your church or your own spiritual life has been dead for some time, don't lose hope! Jesus can resurrect even a body that stinks from decay. Don't limit the power of God with your own thinking and lack of faith. I am convinced that the Lord Jesus can bring you back to life!

Jesus looked up to heaven and prayed to the Father. He then commanded Lazarus, "Come out!" and the dead man walked out of the cave, with linen strips hanging from his body and a cloth still wrapped around his face. Then "Jesus said to them, 'Take off the grave clothes and let him go'" (John 11:44).

My friend, are you tired from years of living your Christian life in your own strength? Do you make your plans and ask God to bless them, rather than seeking out His plans and obeying them? Jesus desires to set you free. He wants you to take off your old grave clothes and exchange them for robes of righteousness.

Your faith may have grown stale and dry, but God wants streams of living water to flow from within you! He wants you to renew your first love and to walk in obedience to Him, realizing He is not only the God of the past and future, but the God of today.

Even if your spiritual life has died and you feel bound with the grave clothes of human endeavour and legalism, then I believe there is still hope for you! Even if you have been in the dark for some time, unable to see the true light of the gospel or feel the warmth of the sun on your face, it is not too late. In the midst of your darkness, if you hear the voice of Jesus calling you to come out, start to walk toward His voice and He will set you free!

I encourage you to kneel down and pour out your heart before the Lord. Allow Him to set you free from your secret sins that have bound you and held you back in chains. If someone has wronged you and you have not forgiven them, now is the time to forgive them from your heart. Unforgiveness and bitterness will cause you to die inside.

It doesn't matter if people reject you and say you are worthless. All that matters is that Jesus loves you, and He wants to be your best friend. Our Lord said:

> *"Greater love has no one than this, that he lay down his life for his friends. You are my friends if you do what I command. I no longer call you servants, because a servant does not know his master's business. Instead, I have called you friends, for everything that I learned from my Father I have made known to you. You did not choose me, but I chose you and appointed you to go and bear fruit—fruit that will last. Then the Father will give you whatever you ask in my name. This is my command: Love each other."*
>
> *John 15:13–17*

You who are loved by Jesus, come out!

True Freedom

"The Spirit of the Lord is on me, because he has anointed me to preach good news to the poor. He has sent me to proclaim freedom for the prisoners and recovery of sight for the blind, to release the oppressed, to proclaim the year of the Lord's favor."

Luke 4:18–19

Soon after God saved me as a teenager, He called me to take the gospel to the West and South. In the first year, I saw more than 3,000 people come to faith in Jesus. There had been such a long famine of the Word of God in China at the time that people's hearts were like tinder boxes. The slightest spark of the Holy Spirit set them ablaze for Jesus! Once the fire of the Holy Spirit ignited them, new believers experienced streams of living water flowing from within them, and the revival spread across China as multitudes of hungry people met the Bread of Life face-to-face.

After a few years, I came to realize that this call God had given me would come at great cost. It was not easy to be a preacher, as every word that came from a preacher's mouth was considered a criminal act by the authorities. They could not control the revival, nor could they understand how the church continued to multiply despite all their efforts to crush or control it.

After my first arrest I was thrown into prison and treated cruelly by the guards and my cellmates. At the beginning I didn't understand what was going on. I was confused and cried out to God, as though there had been some kind of mistake. "Oh Lord," I cried, "do You realize I am sitting here in prison? Have You forsaken me?" Soon the Lord showed me that He had certainly not forsaken me, but that my arrest and imprisonment were His will for my life and His calling for me at that time. The Bible declares that God loves the *entire* world, and Jesus commanded His followers to take the good news into the *entire* world. The world includes Chinese prisons, where there are thousands of desperate men who need to know Jesus. That is where the Lord chose to send me so that I could be a witness to His truth and grace.

When this understanding became a reality in my life, my whole attitude and perspective was completely transformed. Now, instead of feeling resentment for my situation, I was joyful and thankful! Instead of being depressed and confused, I was full of praise to the Lord.

I came to realize that prison is mostly a state of mind rather than a physical place. I learned I can be chained inside a dire prison, surrounded by filth and violence, yet be completely free in my spirit.

Conversely, I have seen that many people's lives in the "free" world are bound and tormented. Millions of people's hearts are tightly chained with sin and addictions, and even though they go to work each day and look like normal people, they are prisoners within. It doesn't matter what they do or where they go, they continue to walk around in a bound and desperate state. Multitudes of people who attend churches are also prisoners. They need the truth of Jesus to set them free!

When the Lord showed me all these things, I made a steadfast commitment that I would always praise Jesus, regardless of my circumstances or situation. I began to worship Him at the top of my voice. On numerous occasions the guards thought I was crazy, but the truth is that I was free, free indeed!

King David also learned the power of praise during his darkest moments. The Psalms record how David worshiped the Lord even though people were plotting to murder him. David understood the power of praising God, even while under tremendous pressure and danger. He was able to declare, "I will bless the LORD at all times: his praise shall continually be in my mouth" (Ps. 34:1 KJV). Later in the same psalm, he dips into his personal experience and shares, "A righteous man may have many troubles, but the LORD delivers him from them all; he protects all his bones, not one of them will be broken" (Ps. 34:19–20).

During the years I spent in prison, I had many times when I felt weak, but it was never too long before the Holy Spirit encouraged me and caused me to sing praises to Jesus. My favorite song was "Praise the Lord! Praise the Lord! Praise Him in the morning. Praise Him in the evening. I will always praise Him!"

Prison was such a dark and depressing place that my sincere joy and positive attitude caught the attention of other prisoners. They knew there was something in me that allowed me to rise above the circumstances, and they wanted to know what it was. This opened countless doors of opportunity to share the gospel, and many of my fellow inmates, as well as guards, were saved by the grace of God.

Whenever you worship Jesus, the presence and glory of God come. When the glory of God comes, everything changes, for "the Lord is the Spirit, and where the Spirit of the Lord is, there is freedom" (2 Cor. 3:17).

The challenges in your life are real, but Jesus is the truth! If you will learn to praise Jesus Christ regardless of your circumstances, you will find inner freedom and joy, and you will have the strength to overcome whatever you are faced with. The joy of the Lord is such a key, because Nehemiah said, "The joy of the LORD is your strength" (Neh. 8:10). If you have allowed the devil to steal the joy of the Lord from you, then you will feel weak and powerless. But when the joy of the Lord returns, you will be strong! If you feel defeated, then "strengthen the feeble hands, steady the knees that give way; say to those with fearful hearts, 'Be strong, do not fear; your God will come'" (Isa. 35:3–4).

It is in the very nature of our God to help the oppressed. The psalmist declared, "He upholds the cause of the oppressed and gives food to the hungry. The LORD sets prisoners free, the LORD gives sight to the blind, the LORD lifts up those who are bowed down, the LORD loves the righteous" (Ps. 146:7–8).

The apostle Paul was another who went through tremendous stress and pressure as he followed God's call on his life, yet he was able to rise above his circumstances because he knew they were just temporary. Jesus is permanent! Paul wrote, "We are hard pressed on every side, but not crushed; perplexed, but not in despair; persecuted, but not abandoned; struck down, but not destroyed. We always carry around in our body the death of Jesus, so that the life of Jesus may also be revealed in our body" (2 Cor. 4:8–10). Paul was even able to describe all of his persecutions and trials as "light and momentary troubles," which were "achieving for us an eternal glory that far outweighs them all. So we fix our eyes not on what is seen, but on what is unseen. For what is seen is temporary, but what is unseen is eternal" (2 Cor. 4:17–18).

I pray you will truly be set free from any prison you find yourself in, whether it is a prison of unbelief, fear or your struggle with sin. Dear friend, don't be condemned, but rather turn to Jesus and be delivered! He wants you to be free, because "if the Son sets you free, you will be free indeed" (John 8:36).

As you set out on this process towards freedom, you need to be honest and realize there will be times when you will be strong and times when you will feel weak.

I faced a new kind of problem after moving to the West. While I was in prison in China, I found it easy to praise the Lord, because everyone hated me except Jesus.

After I started traveling and speaking around the world, however, I found there were many brothers and sisters who clapped and cheered everywhere I spoke, and they always said nice things to me. This was a new kind of temptation – the praise of men. It is a dangerous minefield that every preacher must walk very carefully through, making sure he gives all glory to God and doesn't take any of it into his own heart. To do so brings bondage and a spiritual imprisonment. Jesus said that one of the characteristics of the Pharisees was that "they loved praise from men more than praise from God" (John 12:43).

I have found that the secret to unlocking this freedom in Christ is to praise God wholeheartedly, for "God is spirit, and his worshipers must worship in spirit and in truth" (John 4:24). Whether we are being persecuted and tortured or receiving the adulation of men, the solution is the same – praise and worship of our heavenly Father. The Bible puts it this way: "Through Jesus, therefore, let us continually offer to God a sacrifice of praise – the fruit of lips that confess his name. And do not forget to do good and to share with others, for with such sacrifices God is pleased" (Heb. 13:15–16).

How about you?

Do you face many obstacles in your life that threaten to overwhelm you?

Do you feel crushed and depressed from the weight of life?

Do you feel like the disabled man whom Jesus healed at the Pool of Bethesda? The Bible says he had been an invalid for thirty-eight years, but "when Jesus saw him lying there and learned that he had been in this condition for a long time, he asked him, 'Do you want to get well?'" (John 5:6).

As I travel around, I meet many Christians who have become spiritual invalids. The problems of life have crushed and paralyzed them, and they have spent years being bound by all kinds of diseases – bitterness, unforgiveness, hate, disobedience, jealousy, worldliness, lust and all kinds of addictions. My friend, if this is you, then Jesus also asks you, "Do you want to get well?"

The man at the pool of Bethesda responded to Jesus' question by pouring out all of his frustrations and disappointments: "Sir, I have no one to help me into the pool when the water is stirred. While I am trying to get in, someone else goes down ahead of me" (John 5:7). Jesus listened to the man, just as He will listen to you if you pour out your heart, for "the sacrifices of God are a broken spirit; a broken and contrite heart, O God, you will not despise" (Ps. 51:17).

Not only can Jesus transform and heal your life after years of being bound; He can then take you and use you powerfully as a witness for His kingdom. I believe this is why Jesus told the man to pick up his mat and walk after he was healed. The mat was a sign to people that this man had indeed been an invalid for thirty-eight long years. Here was physical evidence to back up his testimony.

In speaking of the pool of Bethesda, the Bible says, "Here a great number of disabled people used to lie – the blind, the lame, the paralyzed" (John 5:3). If you will open your eyes, you will soon notice there are many blind and lame Christians around you in your community. They have been deeply affected by hopelessness and despair and hounded by past failures. They, too, desperately need the healing touch of Jesus Christ to transform them and make them whole.

When Jesus touches you, His healing is so complete that you can then use your experience to help others who are bound like you were. The Bible puts it this way: "Praise be to the God and Father of our Lord Jesus Christ, the Father of compassion and the God of all comfort, who comforts us in all our troubles, so that we can comfort those in any trouble with the comfort we ourselves have received from God" (2 Cor. 1:3–4).

My friend, you are precious to God. If there are areas of your life where you are bound and captive, bow before Jesus Christ and ask Him to set you free. Get to know the Lord as your best friend, and He will never let you down.

You may experience immediate freedom from some things that have held you back in your life, but other things may require a gradual process as the Holy Spirit teaches you how to overcome the chains that have kept you captive for so long and how to walk in victory over sin. None of us are such superhuman Christians that we experience a victorious life twenty-four hours a day. The key thing is that you allow Jesus to take you by the hand and lead you on the path to freedom.

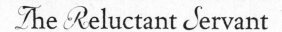

9

The Reluctant Servant

Jonah was a reluctant servant of God. He received God's calling to be a prophet to Nineveh, but he chose to ignore the Lord and go his own way.

When the Lord told Jonah to go to Nineveh to warn them of impending judgment, it didn't suit Jonah's schedule! Jonah was just like many Christians today – they have their lives planned out for the next year and are so inflexible that even if God tells them to do something, they are unwilling to interrupt their precious schedules. Jesus taught, "Do not worry about tomorrow, for tomorrow will worry about itself. Each day has enough trouble of its own" (Matt. 6:34).

Jonah means "dove." For a time, this dove lost his direction. God told him to go to Nineveh, which is in present-day Iraq, but instead he went in the opposite direction, to Tarshish, which some Bible scholars believe to be in present-day Spain. Jonah started his journey on the eastern end of the Mediterranean Sea and was trying to flee to the furthermost region at the western end of the sea, a trip that would have taken weeks.

It is never a good idea to put your own plans ahead of God's plan for your life. Doing so is guaranteed to end in disaster and pain. Rather, the Bible tells us to humble ourselves and submit all our plans to God's will. "Trust in the LORD with all your heart and lean not on your own understanding; in all your ways acknowledge him, and he will make your paths straight" (Prov. 3:5–6). Conversely, when we lean on our own understanding, our path becomes very crooked.

Not only did Jonah put himself in danger, but all the other people with him on the boat were also placed in great danger. It is not good for anyone when a child of God rebels against God's commands. Others nearby may also be hurt. Jonah was thrown overboard by the crew of the ship, and as you know, he ended up inside the belly of a huge fish.

If you belong to Jesus Christ, then you are His servant and you no longer have the right to control and plan your own life. The Bible clearly says, "You are not your own; you were bought at a price. Therefore honor God with your body" (1 Cor. 6:19–20). Everybody in the world is a slave. Either they are slaves of Jesus Christ, or they are slaves to sin. It is better to belong to Jesus! Whereas earthly masters love to dominate and subdue their subjects, Jesus says, "Come to me, all you who are weary and burdened, and I will give you rest. Take my yoke upon you and learn from me, for I am gentle and humble in heart, and you will find rest for your souls. For my yoke is easy and my burden is light" (Matt. 11:28–30).

In my life I have disobeyed God at certain times, and on each occasion my disobedience resulted in pain. In 2001 I was in the country of Myanmar, preparing to bring my wife and children out to Germany. The Holy Spirit warned me not to carry our Burmese identity cards with me when I left the country, but I disobeyed and took them along. The cards had not been issued through proper official channels, and the end result was that I was arrested, beaten and sentenced to seven years in prison.

Just after my arrest I reminded the Lord that He had previously delivered me from prison in China through a series of miracles, and I invited Him to do the same again. Then I realized that this situation was completely different. In China I had been arrested for the sake of the gospel, but in Myanmar I had been arrested because of my pride and disobedience to the Lord. When this realization struck me, I was full of deep remorse and grief. I cried out from the depths of my heart, asking God to forgive and cleanse me of my sin. Praise be to our Lord, because "if we confess our sins, he is faithful and just and will forgive us our sins and purify us from all unrighteousness" (1 John 1:9).

Jesus forgave me and restored me to right fellowship with the heavenly Father.

Jonah also found himself in deep trouble, for God had created a special fish and placed it in the Mediterranean Sea. For years that huge fish swam around, waiting to fulfill the purpose God had for it. One day the Spirit of the Lord moved upon the fish and caused it to open its mouth and swallow a reluctant servant of God!

No doubt while he was trapped inside the dark belly of the fish for three days and three nights, Jonah pondered the events that had brought about the predicament he found himself in. With all the stomach acids sloshing around him and the unbearable stench, Jonah must have felt like he was stuck inside a giant washing machine! God had found a way to become the priority in Jonah's schedule: the Bible records that "from inside the fish Jonah prayed to the Lord his God. He said: 'In my distress I called to the Lord, and he answered me. From the depths of the grave I called for help, and you listened to my cry' " (Jonah 2:1–2).

God heard Jonah's sincere prayer and "commanded the fish, and it vomited Jonah onto dry land" (2:10). Jonah would have had no idea where he was. Perhaps he thought, "Good. After traveling for three days and nights, perhaps I am now in Tarshish." I have found that when we disobey God, He doesn't gloss over our indiscretion but always brings us back to the place where we will have another chance to obey. As Jonah was wiping his eyes and trying to gain his bearings, "the word of the LORD came to Jonah a second time: 'Go to the great city of Nineveh and proclaim to it the message I give you.' Jonah obeyed the word of the LORD and went to Nineveh" (3:1–3).

Similarly, God did a miracle for me in Myanmar by giving me a second chance to obey. He allowed me to go free after seven months and seven days of my seven-year sentence, and during the time of my incarceration, He allowed me to lead a number of prisoners to faith in Christ. Then, on the day the Lord appointed, I was suddenly vomited out of prison and out of Myanmar and reunited with my family. God is good!

Over the years, some people have told me that God has called them to a beautiful island or to the warm climate of Florida or other such idyllic locations. Now if God really calls us to a place where we feel comfortable, then we are very fortunate indeed. But what if God calls you to a place that you would rather die than go to?

What if you pray tonight and the small, still voice of the Holy Spirit says to you, "My child, I want you to go to Baghdad and witness about my Son to the Iraqis"? What if God sends you somewhere abhorrent to you so that every fiber in your being revolts against the very thought of it?

Before we are too quick to judge Jonah, we need to realize that this is what happened to him. Nineveh at the time was the most violent, demonized place in the world. The people there had cruelly oppressed the Israelites for generations, and Jonah was not prepared to take a message from God to them. He felt they deserved to be destroyed and wiped off the face of the earth. Jonah knew that God was merciful and forgiving, and he didn't want the people of Nineveh to have a chance to repent. Listen to Jonah's remarkable words: "O LORD, is this not what I said when I was still at home? That is why I was so quick to flee to Tarshish. I knew that you are a gracious and compassionate God, slow to anger and abounding in love, a God who relents from sending calamity" (4:2).

This, of course, is just the point. None of us deserve God's salvation! It is only by the grace of God that any of us find Jesus Christ. The apostle Paul pointed this out when he wrote:

> As for you, you were dead in your transgressions and sins, in which you used to live when you followed the ways of this world and of the ruler of the kingdom of the air, the spirit who is now at work in those who are disobedient. All of us also lived among them at one time, gratifying the cravings of our sinful nature and following its desires and thoughts. Like the rest, we were by nature objects of wrath. But because of his great love for us, God, who is rich in mercy, made us alive with Christ even when we were dead in transgressions—it is by grace you have been saved.
>
> Ephesians 2:1–5

It is a false kind of Christianity that teaches God only wants us to be safe and secure and to keep out of harm's way. I have seen that many missionary organizations do not send their workers into any country where they may be at risk. This approach will never win the world for Jesus! Wherever there is a stronghold of Satan, the messengers of Jesus Christ will be strongly opposed, attacked and, if God allows it, put to death. It is not to safe locations that we should go, but to wherever God commands us. If it costs our lives, then good, for we will get to heaven sooner.

The only place in the world "too dangerous" for the disciple of Jesus Christ is the place of being outside of God's will. He does not expect His followers just to live in peace with everyone. In fact, the opposite is true, for the gospel is an abrasive message that confronts sin and evil head-on. Jesus said, "Do not suppose that I have come to bring peace to the earth. I did not come to bring peace, but a sword. For I have come to turn 'a man against his father, a daughter against her mother, a daughter-in-law against her mother-in-law—a man's enemies will be the members of his own household'" (Matt. 10:34–36).

The true gospel, when it is preached with power, always results in either revival or riot. Just read Paul's experiences in the book of Acts.

Did you ever consider that Jesus sent His own followers on suicide missions? He knew His disciples would be killed as they attempted to take the gospel throughout the world. This realization did not prevent Jesus from commanding His followers to go forth and die for His kingdom! He told them, "If you belonged to the world, it would love you as its own. As it is, you do not belong to the world, but I have chosen you out of the world. That is why the world hates you. Remember the words I spoke to you: 'No servant is greater than his master.' If they persecuted me, they will persecute you also. If they obeyed my teaching, they will obey yours also. They will treat you this way because of my name, for they do not know the One who sent me" (John 15:19–21).

These days there are too many Christians with conditions attached to their faith. They tell God where and when He can speak to them, what kind of things He can say, and which commands they are willing to obey and which they will ignore.

Such "faith" is no faith at all, and God will judge such self-centered people if they refuse to change. The good news is that you can change. Our loving heavenly Father has clearly laid out what we must do to put Jesus at the center of our lives again and to have the ability to discern His will: "Therefore, I urge you, brothers, in view of God's mercy, to offer your bodies as living sacrifices, holy and pleasing to God – this is your spiritual act of worship. Do not conform any longer to the pattern of this world, but be transformed by the renewing of your mind. Then you will be able to test and approve what God's will is – his good, pleasing and perfect will" (Rom. 12:1–2).

If we belong to God, we must learn to put our own schedules away. We must bundle up all of our hopes, dreams and future plans and lay them at the feet of Jesus. Even our very bodies, the Scriptures say, should be offered as living sacrifices. Such faith is holy and acceptable in God's sight.

Now you may be reading this and your mind is recoiling at the thought of making such a radical commitment and abandonment to God's will. Somehow we deceive ourselves into thinking that if we retain control of our lives, things will be okay, and we fear that if we truly give our lives to God, we will regret it. This thinking is completely false. Nobody who has ever given control of their life to Jesus has regretted it.

Oh, if we would have a revelation of God's care and provision for His children, we would never be the same again! He is much better at running your life than you are! "Humble yourselves, therefore, under God's mighty hand, that he may lift you up in due time. Cast all your anxiety on him because he cares for you" (1 Peter 5:6–7).

Jonah surrendered to God's will and arrived in the wicked city of Nineveh. When he opened his mouth, the Holy Spirit spoke through him so powerfully that the entire city humbled themselves and repented! "The Ninevites believed God. They declared a fast, and all of them, from the greatest to the least, put on sackcloth. When the news reached the king of Nineveh, he rose from his throne, took off his royal robes, covered himself with sackcloth and sat down in the dust. Then he issued a proclamation in Nineveh: 'By the decree of the king and his nobles: Do not let any man or beast, herd or flock, taste anything; do not let them eat or drink. But let man and beast be covered with sackcloth. Let everyone call urgently on God. Let them give up their evil ways and their violence. Who knows? God may yet relent and with compassion turn from his fierce anger so that we will not perish'" (Jonah 3:5–9).

The story of Jonah does not end when Nineveh repented, however. When Jonah saw that God had compassion on the wicked city, he was angry! Jonah didn't want God to reach that place to begin with. He felt they were undeserving of salvation and was disappointed when God relented from bringing disaster. Jonah was so angry at the Lord's compassion that he prayed, "Now, O LORD, take away my life, for it is better for me to die than to live" (4:3).

Jonah delivered his message with a terrible attitude, yet God "was pleased through the foolishness of what was preached to save those who believe" (1 Cor. 1:21). There is no evidence that

Jonah ever bothered to learn the language of the Ninevites. Perhaps they had to find a translator to understand what he was saying. He reluctantly spoke the message God had told him to, and the Holy Spirit did the rest! When you speak for God, realize it is not your own wise or persuasive words that matter, but the power of God operating through you. Paul said, "My message and my preaching were not with wise and persuasive words, but with a demonstration of the Spirit's power, so that your faith might not rest on men's wisdom, but on God's power" (1 Cor. 2:4–5).

If you have God's call upon your life but want to bring the result to pass in your own way, you will miss the glory, and you will miss the miracles of God. I have met many pastors who have spent decades in the ministry, and while they do everything imaginable to keep their ministry moving, they have missed their main calling to follow the Lord in His power and might and to obey Him regardless of the cost. God's work is accomplished " 'not by might nor by power, but by my Spirit,' says the Lord Almighty" (Zech. 4:6).

The story of Jonah concludes with the prophet still angry at God. He slumped down on the ground outside the city and constructed a makeshift shelter so he could sit and watch God obliterate Nineveh. After all, Jonah's message had been very simple: "If you don't repent, God will destroy you within forty days!" He found himself a place a safe distance outside the city where he could watch the show. Jonah was probably expecting fire and brimstone to fall from the skies and demolish the city like God had destroyed Sodom and Gomorrah.

Our loving God provided a vine to grow over Jonah's shelter to shade him from the blistering sun. The next day, however, God sent a worm that ate the vine, and a scorching wind that withered it. Jonah felt faint and again complained to God that he would rather die than go through this miserable experience. The response from the Lord reveals His kind and loving heart. Remember that Nineveh was a wicked, violent city that had persecuted the Israelites for generations, but the Lord told Jonah, "You have been concerned about this vine, though you did not tend it or make it grow. It sprang up overnight and died overnight. But Nineveh has more than a hundred and twenty thousand people who cannot tell their right hand from their left, and many cattle as well. Should I not be concerned about that great city?" (Jonah 4:10–11).

Dear friend, please realize that God has a plan to reach every part of the world because He loves people and desires that none of them would perish. He wishes everyone would come to repentance and put their faith in His Son. Don't start thinking that God should wipe Muslims off the face of the earth because of their violence and unbelief. A day is coming when all the nations will be judged, but in the meantime the Holy Spirit is working to bring lost people out of the Devil's clutches. God's will is that the one billion Muslims of the world – and all other people – will "open their eyes and turn ... from darkness to light, and from the power of Satan to God, so that they may receive forgiveness of sins and a place among those who are sanctified by faith in me" (Acts 26:18).

If you find yourself trapped in darkness because of disobedience to God, there is no time to waste. Repent and confess your sins to Him. "Repent, then, and turn to God, so that your sins may be wiped out, that times of refreshing may come from the Lord, and that he may send the Christ, who has been appointed for you – even Jesus" (Acts 3:19–20).

Let us humble ourselves and ask God to give us His heart

for the nations, lest we, like Jonah, become reluctant servants. On the day that Jesus returns, may we hear those blessed words, "Well done, good and faithful servant! You have been faithful with a few things; I will put you in charge of many things. Come and share your master's happiness!" (Matt. 25:21).

Part 2

Streams of Living Water

10

As Bold as a Lion

The wicked man flees though no one pursues, but the righteous are as bold as a lion.

Proverbs 28:1

There are many timid Christians today, but the two words "timid" and "Christian" do not belong together. To be a Christian means to be like Christ, and He is full of God's fire and passion. Jesus was not timid when He confronted the Pharisees, tackled sin and denounced the rulers of the day. He was not timid when He overturned the tables of the money-changers in the temple courts. Nothing about Jesus is timid. He boldly went through torture on the cross for you and me, and "having disarmed principalities and powers, He made a public spectacle of them, triumphing over them in it" (Col. 2:15 NKJV).

The boldness of Jesus was motivated and driven by His love for God and people and by His desire to obey the Father. Our boldness should be motivated by these same things and should not just be some kind of human bravado that we try to conjure up.

The kind of boldness that pleases God comes about when

the Holy Spirit flows into your life. Before receiving the power of the Holy Spirit, Peter boldly declared, "Even if I have to die with you, I will never disown you" (Mark 14:31). This statement came not from the boldness God gives; rather, Peter made a statement of human bravado, which counts for nothing. That same night Peter denied Jesus three times. On the day of Pentecost, however, Peter was filled with the Holy Spirit and became a courageous preacher. He was given the honor of being the first preacher at the dawn of the church, and 3,000 people were saved on the very first day.

How is it that terrorists are willing to strap explosives to their chests and die for Satan, while many Christians are as timid as a mouse and afraid to witness to their neighbors? When we are timid and too afraid to obey Jesus, the results are all bad. As sons and daughters of the living God, we have the power of the gospel. Have we done everything possible to take the gospel to the Muslim extremists who are now attacking the West? Brother Andrew of Open Doors has said, "If you do not go to the heathen with the gospel, they will come to you as revolutionaries or as occupying forces."

When the Holy Spirit enters your heart and takes over, you will not be afraid, for a holy fire of God's love will consume you. You will not be the same person as before, and fear will vanish, for "there is no fear in love. But perfect love drives out fear, because fear has to do with punishment. The one who fears is not made perfect in love. We love because he first loved us" (1 John 4:18–19).

The Bible is full of bold people doing bold acts of faith for God. It was surely bold when Noah decided to obey God and build a huge boat even though there was no evidence that God would destroy the earth with water. Noah boldly continued the work, despite the mocking and laughter of everyone who heard about it. The New Testament records, "By faith Noah, when warned about things not yet seen, in holy fear built an ark to save his family. By his faith he condemned the world and became heir of the righteousness that comes by faith" (Heb. 11:7).

It took boldness for the children of Israel to step down into the Red Sea and pass through on dry ground, with walls of water piled up on both sides of them.

It took great courage from God for a succession of prophets to boldly speak out for God in the face of continual attacks, imprisonment, slander and hardship.

David was empowered with God's heavenly boldness as he ran towards the fully armed Goliath with nothing more than five small stones and a sling in his hand. David reasoned that God would do a miracle, and he was willing to put his life on the line to see it. David said, "When I called, you answered me; you made me bold and stouthearted" (Ps. 138:3).

One of the greatest acts of courage and boldness recorded in the Scriptures took place when Jonathan and his young armor bearer took on the whole Philistine army by themselves! They scrambled up a cliff while the enemy looked on. The Bible does not record the name of the armor bearer, but he too was clearly filled with the boldness of the Holy Spirit. Jonathan had said to him, "Come, let's go over to the outpost of those uncircumcised fellows. Perhaps the LORD will act in our behalf. Nothing can hinder the LORD from saving, whether by many or by few" (1 Sam. 14:6). The armor bearer had just been asked to put his life on the line and join Jonathan in single-handedly attacking a large army. Remarkably, he told Jonathan, "Do all that you have in mind. Go ahead; I am with you heart and soul" (1 Sam. 14:7).

God loves such boldness when it is based on His glory and the advance of His kingdom. It moves Him, and He always answers from heaven. On this occasion, "panic struck the whole army—those in the camp and field, and those in the outposts and raiding parties—and the ground shook. It was a panic sent by God" (1 Sam. 14:15). This act of boldness by Jonathan and his armor bearer brought a great victory for Israel, and the enemy was routed.

The apostle Paul was also a very bold man. After he met Jesus on the road to Damascus, Paul was dramatically changed and became as bold as a lion. He declared, "I am not ashamed of the gospel, because it is the power of God for the salvation of everyone who believes" (Rom. 1:16).

To be bold witnesses for the Lord Jesus, we first need to empty ourselves and depend on the Lord to change and empower us. When Peter and John stood before the Sanhedrin, they boldly proclaimed the gospel and exhorted the rulers to repent and put their faith in Jesus. Their fearlessness took the Sanhedrin aback, and the Bible records, "When they saw the courage of Peter and John and realized that they were unschooled, ordinary men, they were astonished and they took note that these men had been with Jesus" (Acts 4:13).

If you are a bold Christian, then people likewise should not think it is something you have obtained by your own efforts and determination, but they should realize your boldness is a by-product of your relationship with Jesus.

After being released from prison, Peter and John returned to the other believers and reported what had taken place. The church rose up and prayed, " 'Now, Lord, consider their threats

and enable your servants to speak your word with great boldness. Stretch out your hand to heal and perform miraculous
signs and wonders through the name of your holy servant
Jesus.' After they prayed, the place where they were meeting
was shaken. And they were all filled with the Holy Spirit and
spoke the word of God boldly" (Acts 4:29–31).

Paul asked the Ephesians to pray for him so that "whenever
I open my mouth, words may be given me so that I will fearlessly make known the mystery of the gospel, for which I am
an ambassador in chains. Pray that I may declare it fearlessly,
as I should" (Eph. 6:19–20).

The book of Acts records the results of Paul's boldness. On
one occasion he "entered the synagogue and spoke boldly there
for three months, arguing persuasively about the kingdom of
God" (Acts 19:8); and later, "for two whole years Paul stayed
there in his own rented house and welcomed all who came to
see him. Boldly and without hindrance he preached the kingdom of God and taught about the Lord Jesus Christ" (Acts
28:30–31).

I know of a believer in China who managed to escape from
prison. He had been horribly tortured and mistreated, and his
escape was a miracle from God. Despite the cruel treatment
he had received, within a few days of his escape, this brother
started to miss the close fellowship he had enjoyed with other
Christians in the prison. He was concerned about their welfare
and longed to encourage them to stand firm in the faith.

Even though he had just escaped from prison and the authorities were searching everywhere for him, this man boldly
decided to return to the prison as a visitor, in order to see his
brothers in Christ and momentarily encourage them. He went
to the prison gates and handed over his identity card, which

showed his real name. His request to see a certain prisoner was processed, and in due time the inmate was brought out of the cell. What a surprise he received when he saw that his visitor was none other than his own cellmate who had escaped just a few days earlier!

Trying not to show too much excitement, the prisoner and his bold visitor enjoyed a few minutes of fellowship. They exhorted one another to remain firm in Christ and to continue to boldly preach the gospel to everyone.

The visitation time came to an end, and the visitor calmly thanked the guards, took his identity card back, and walked out into the street. Just moments later—as if God lifted a cloud from their minds—the guards realized that the visitor was none other than the escapee they had been searching the city for! They raced out into the street with their guns drawn, but the man could not be found.

Some people would say it was stupid for that man to return to the prison he had just escaped from, but I believe the love of God compelled him to attempt such a bold act. He reasoned that the benefits of being able to encourage his brother in Christ outweighed the risk of being arrested again. "If we are out of our mind, it is for the sake of God; if we are in our right mind, it is for you. For Christ's love compels us, because we are convinced that one died for all, and therefore all died. And he died for all, that those who live should no longer live for themselves but for him who died for them and was raised again" (2 Cor. 5:13–15).

Heavenly boldness and courage marked the lives of many men and women in the Bible. They were not bold or courageous in themselves—indeed, many were weak and timid before God transformed their lives—but when they humbled themselves, God's mighty power lifted them up and caused them to perform many great deeds.

How about you?

Have you ever experienced the boldness and courage of the Holy Spirit surging inside of you, causing you to do the impossible for God? Have you ever stepped out on a limb to serve the Lord, or has your Christianity been largely a "private" affair, characterized by keeping your faith to yourself and living at a "safe distance" from God?

Are you afraid to tell others about Jesus Christ and the transformation He can bring to their lives? Or are you worried those people might embarrass and ridicule you for your faith? You see, true boldness can never come to those who have not yet died to self. People who have already died don't care what others think or say about them. Dead people don't worry about their reputation or whether people will look down on them.

If you want to make a difference for God's kingdom, you first must learn to die to yourself. This is not just a onetime experience, but a daily necessity. Jesus said, "If anyone would come after me, he must deny himself and take up his cross daily and follow me. For whoever wants to save his life will lose it, but whoever loses his life for me will save it" (Luke 9:23–24). Paul told the Corinthians, "I die every day—I mean that, brothers—just as surely as I glory over you in Christ Jesus our Lord" (1 Cor. 15:31).

The kingdom of God does not advance in this world through human endeavour. It advances through the life of Jesus Christ flowing through His servants who have died to themselves and their own desires. Peter explained, "Since Christ suffered in his body, arm yourselves also with the same attitude, because he who has suffered in his body is done with sin. As a result, he does not live the rest of his earthly life for evil human desires, but rather for the will of God" (1 Peter 4:1–2).

The will of God should be the primary focus of all Christians. To glorify Him should be our greatest honor and privilege. All else is a waste of time, and this world is perishing while too many Christians live out fleshly lives full of compromise and selfishness.

The good news is that our Lord is loving and merciful, and He will forgive all who come to Him in humility and meekness. He can take your life and make you as bold as a lion and bring your days as a timid Christian to an end. Are you willing to submit to this process of being daily shaped and molded by the Holy Spirit?

If you are, you will not regret it.

A long time ago there was a timid young man named Gideon. Because of the circumstances around him, he was deeply discouraged. The enemy forces were so strong that the Israelites frequently hid in caves and in the mountains. When the angel of the Lord found Gideon, he brought a message that went directly against all common sense at the time: "When the angel of the LORD appeared to Gideon, he said, 'The LORD is with you, mighty warrior'" (Judg. 6:12).

Gideon must have thought the angel was referring to someone else! He was living under the oppression of the Midianites, and the last thing in the world he felt like was a mighty warrior. Gideon even told the angel that "the LORD has abandoned us and put us into the hand of Midian" (Judg. 6:13).

Gideon had lost his sense of perspective. He was full of fear and hopelessness and could only see his failures.

Do you feel like Gideon?

You may have been a timid and fearful person in the past,

but God wants you to hand your fears to Him and become as bold as a lion. You see, it doesn't matter at all how people see you or what they say about you. It doesn't even matter what you think about yourself.

All that matters is how God sees you.

What God says about you is the truth, and the truth will set you free.

When God says you are a mighty warrior, then you *are* a mighty warrior.

When God says you can do it, you *can* do it!

When God says that He has "raised us up with Christ and seated us with him in the heavenly realms in Christ Jesus" (Eph. 2:6), it is true, whether you feel like it or not. Don't pay attention to those people who discourage you and tell you what you can't do. Instead, "let God be true, and every man a liar" (Rom. 3:4).

I exhort you in Christ: please do not forget your identity. You are a redeemed one, chosen by the almighty God to be His child. Your heavenly Father wants you to be a bold warrior who depends on His mighty power. He wants you to be as bold as a lion. Amen!

$\mathscr{V}$essels of $\mathscr{R}$efreshment

> But we have this treasure in jars of clay to show that
> this all-surpassing power is from God and not from us.
>
> *2 Corinthians 4:7*

$\mathscr{T}$hese are exciting days we are living in. God is doing mighty things in many parts of the world where there had previously been no light of the gospel. This good news does not get reported on your television or in the newspapers, as the media tends to report mostly the bad news of the world. Yet God is saving millions of people and completely transforming their lives from the inside out. "All over the world this gospel is bearing fruit and growing, just as it has been doing among you since the day you heard it and understood God's grace in all its truth" (Col. 1:6).

A number of years ago the Lord showed the house church leaders in China to launch an initiative called the "gospel month." Between Christmas and Chinese New Year, every believer was required to lead at least three people to faith in Jesus Christ and then begin to disciple and train them, in turn, to go out and win more people to the Lord. Each church leader was required to lead and disciple at least five people during this time. The results were extraordinary. In my home area of Nanyang alone, more than 12,000 new believers were baptized in a single day. They were then trained, and the following year, approximately 300,000 people came to the Lord in Nanyang! In the years since the gospel month was launched, it has spread to many other parts of China and whole regions have been saturated with the gospel. Millions of people have been saved, and the church has been a vessel of refreshment for the kingdom of God.

God wants to bring His living water to your nation too, but you need to first realize that the living water will not flow directly from heaven, nor will it flow from your church buildings, for the Lord said that streams of living water would flow from within *us*! Before your nation will see a revival, the followers of Jesus Christ must first experience a revival in their own lives. Only then will the water be able to flow out and bring refreshment to others.

The very first miracle Jesus did involved water. The Lord was invited to attend a wedding in the village of Cana, on the shore of the Sea of Galilee. When the wine had run out, the Lord's mother instructed the servants to do whatever Jesus told them to do. The Bible records, "Nearby stood six stone water jars, the kind used by the Jews for ceremonial washing, each holding from twenty to thirty gallons. Jesus said to the servants, 'Fill the jars with water'; so they filled them to the brim" (John 2:6–7).

The first thing to note is that these six large jars were normally used for ceremonial washing, as the Jews were required to be clean before worshiping God. No doubt, over time, these jars started to become worn and grimy. Perhaps a crust had built up around the rims.

This speaks of the condition of many Christians today. Their lives are designed to bring fresh water and blessing to those around them, but due to years of overuse, they start to lose contact with the living water of the Holy Spirit. The vessel that was created to bring refreshment to God's people can become contaminated. It is a terrible thing to meet Christians in such a condition. You can easily recognize them by the constant criticism and gossip that come from their lips.

Brothers and sisters, God has a better way. If you have become a contaminated vessel, burdened with the cares of the world, then I have good news! Jesus loves you, and He wants you to cast all your cares on Him. Repent, and He will forgive you and receive you back into His fold. The Bible says, "Humble yourselves, therefore, under God's mighty hand, that he may lift you up in due time. Cast all your anxiety on him because he cares for you" (1 Peter 5:6–7).

Jesus never asked you to carry the burdens of the world on your shoulders. Only He can do that. He wants to say to you, "Come to me, all you who are weary and burdened, and I will give you rest. Take my yoke upon you and learn from me, for I am gentle and humble in heart, and you will find rest for your souls. For my yoke is easy and my burden is light" (Matt. 11:28–30).

An overburdened Christian will never be able to experience the streams of living water flowing from within. Let's spend time with Jesus and lay down those things that He never asked us to carry.

As you know, Jesus turned the water inside those six large jars into the most delicious wine anybody had tasted. The master of the banquet was puzzled that the best wine had not been brought out first. He said, " 'Everyone brings out the choice wine first and then the cheaper wine after the guests have had too much to drink; but you have saved the best till now.' This, the first of his miraculous signs, Jesus performed at Cana in Galilee. He thus revealed his glory, and his disciples put their faith in him" (John 2:10–11).

How was it that Jesus "revealed his glory" by turning this water into wine? I believe it is because He reversed the natural order of things. Being God, He is able to reverse the natural laws of the universe. After all, He created it! He alone was able to take water from an old jar and transform it into delicious wine.

In the same way, Jesus can take your tired and stained life and completely transform you into a vessel of refreshment! Only Jesus can reverse the natural decay of your life. Religion cannot do it, nor can your own efforts do it. Only Jesus can change you from the inside out! God wants to "bestow on them a crown of beauty instead of ashes, the oil of gladness instead of mourning, and a garment of praise instead of a spirit of despair. They will be called oaks of righteousness, a planting of the LORD for the display of his splendor" (Isa. 61:3).

God wants His children to be vessels full of living water. If you have family members who don't know Jesus, I pray you will be the vessel that brings the living water into their lives. Water is such a wonderful blessing. Without it our world would quickly come to an end.

Jesus has an endless supply of living water for us to use in this life. We only have these few days on the earth to reach out to the lost and dying world. All those who perish without having tasted the living water of the Holy Spirit will never have a chance to drink again. Jesus told a harrowing story of a rich man who was being tormented in hell. "He looked up and saw

Abraham far away, with Lazarus by his side. So he called to him, 'Father Abraham, have pity on me and send Lazarus to dip the tip of his finger in water and cool my tongue, because I am in agony in this fire.' But Abraham replied, 'Son, remember that in your lifetime you received your good things, while Lazarus received bad things, but now he is comforted here and you are in agony'" (Luke 16:23–25).

Oh, friends, let us realize that we must be vessels filled with living water to refresh people in this life, lest they spend eternity in a place without a single drop of water. This generation is in desperate condition. Whether they realize it or not, they crave the living water of God. They are sick and tired of dead religion and rituals, for they know that these things do not quench the thirst in their hearts. No wonder there are thousands of churches with few believers in them. I have been in huge cathedrals in Europe where only a handful of old ladies attend the services. Thirsty people are not stupid. They quickly know if your church is a source of living water or not. You might claim to walk with Jesus and be partakers of His life, but people will soon leave your church for elsewhere if all they get served is a crusty old piece of bread.

Multitudes of church leaders feed their flocks not from the reservoir of God's living water, but from the dark cisterns of dead theological training and human reasoning. No wonder so many Christians are spiritually sick and constipated! Christians who have received visions and dreams to serve God soon lose their focus in such a cruel environment. Their enthusiasm and dreams are crushed by people who are like Joseph's brothers, who said, "Come now, let's kill him and throw him into one of these cisterns and say that a ferocious animal devoured him. Then we'll see what comes of his dreams" (Gen. 37:20).

It's a dreadful thing to live your life in your own strength instead of God's, and to ignore the living water He offers in favor of building your own cisterns. " 'Be appalled at this, O heavens, and shudder with great horror,' declares the LORD. 'My people have committed two sins: They have forsaken me, the spring of living water, and have dug their own cisterns, broken cisterns that cannot hold water' " (Jer. 2:12–13).

It's time for us to stop playing religious games with God. It's time to get serious. It's no longer good enough just to "believe" in Jesus; we need to become His disciples. Churches should not be places where we come and get the water inside of us drained out. Rather, churches should be staging posts from where living water flows out into the communities and nations of the world.

If the living water God has given you remains locked inside, it soon becomes stagnant. Stagnant water is dangerous and can carry disease. The living water must be replenished daily so that it can flow out to others. Don't think that just because you have been filled with the Holy Spirit once that it is enough. The Holy Spirit should continually fill and overflow you. When this happens you will start to see miracles and many people coming to salvation, just as in the Bible.

I want to share with you the key secret for how Christians can experience a continual flow of living water in their lives. In my opinion, this key is the one major thing missing in the Western church and among sections of the body of Christ in other parts of the world.

The answer to experiencing God's living water is *not* to seek more and more Bible teaching.

The answer is *not* to attend more Christian conferences or seek new ministers with new messages.

Please listen carefully. The key for experiencing the flow of God's living water in your life is ...

Obedience.

Most Christians I have met in the Western world have plenty of Bible knowledge, but they do not experience the living water flowing from their lives because of their disobedience.

God doesn't want you to know everything and do nothing.

He would rather you know a little and act on that little in obedience, and then He will give you more.

We need to come to Jesus again and again for living water, but not if we plan to keep it for our own benefit and edification. God wants us to start obeying what He commanded us to do. We need to get off our backsides and "go and make disciples of all nations, baptizing them in the name of the Father and of the Son and of the Holy Spirit, and teaching them to obey everything I have commanded you" (Matt. 28:19–20).

I am not at all suggesting that you should sign up for more of your church's programs or get busier than you already are, performing "Christian activities". These will not cause the living water to overflow in your life! What I'm talking about is that you completely surrender to Jesus Christ and be willing to serve and obey Him regardless of where it takes you. Only then will you discover the plan that God has for your life. As you take Jesus by the hand and step out in faith, He will bless you in such a marvelous way that living water will spill over and enable His life to flow to others around you.

I am not talking about obeying the Great Commission merely by paying more attention to your missionaries' newsletters pinned to the notice board of your church. Nor do I mean that you should sign up to be involved in a local initiative. These may be starting points, but when you seriously dedicate your life to doing whatever God wants to make the name of Jesus known throughout the earth, and you begin to follow the leading of the Holy Spirit, then you will begin to find your life overflowing with living water. It will then flow to your family, your church and the community God has called you to reach. You will be a vessel of God's blessings that will bring refreshment to both the church and the world. Whole nations can be flooded by the presence of Jesus. We have seen this in China, and other parts of the world have seen it happen too.

In the next chapter we will look further at what the Bible says about streams of living water, but first we need to be willing to submit ourselves to God's process so that we become vessels of refreshment.

Dear friend, are you a follower of Christ who has lost touch with the source of the living water that Jesus promised His disciples?

Has your heart become hard and your spiritual life little more than a dreary, burdensome chore? Is it only on rare occasions that you experience the joy of the Lord in your life?

I have good news for you. Hear what the Lord says about His sheep: "I will bless them and the places surrounding my hill. I will send down showers in season; there will be showers of blessing. The trees of the field will yield their fruit and the ground will yield its crops; the people will be secure in their land. They will know that I am the LORD, when I break the bars of their yoke and rescue them from the hands of those who enslaved them" (Ezek. 34:26–27).

If this all seems overwhelming to you, then just relax and remember that Jesus wants to take your burdens, not add to them. If the soil of your heart has become hard and dry, I encourage you, dear friend, to confess your sins to our heavenly

Father and cry out for His help. The Holy Spirit will start to change you by moistening your hard heart. Remember that God desires an intimate relationship with you, and He loves you more than you can imagine. Let's conclude with the beautiful words of Hosea 10:12:

> *Sow for yourselves righteousness,*
> *reap the fruit of unfailing love,*
> *and break up your unplowed ground;*
> *for it is time to seek the LORD,*
> *until he comes*
> *and showers righteousness on you.*

12

Streams of Living Water

> On the last and greatest day of the Feast, Jesus stood and said in a loud voice, "If anyone is thirsty, let him come to me and drink. Whoever believes in me, as the Scripture has said, streams of living water will flow from within him." By this he meant the Spirit, whom those who believed in him were later to receive.
>
> *John 7:37-39*

What a marvelous privilege we have as sons and daughters of God! Jesus promised that "streams of living water" would flow from within us. Have you experienced this in your own life? We need more of God's presence in our lives, because I know that when these streams of living water start to flow from within us, not only will the barren wilderness be transformed into bountiful life, but the forces of darkness will be toppled and swept away!

Did you know the Devil has a counterfeit stream? His stream brings death and destruction wherever it flows. It spews forth impurities, terror and everything that is opposed to the glorious gospel of Jesus Christ. Our Lord doesn't abandon us to be swept away, however. The Word of God states that "when the enemy comes in like a flood, the Spirit of the LORD will lift up a standard against him" (Isa. 59:19 NKJV).

Indeed, Satan even tried to sweep Jesus away with a dirty river of death: "When the dragon saw that he had been hurled to the earth, he pursued the woman who had given birth to the male child.... Then from his mouth the serpent spewed water like a river, to overtake the woman and sweep her away with the torrent. But the earth helped the woman by opening its mouth and swallowing the river that the dragon had spewed out of his mouth. Then the dragon was enraged at the woman and went off to make war against the rest of her offspring – those who obey God's commandments and hold to the testimony of Jesus" (Rev. 12:13, 15–17).

Are you one of those who obeys God's commands and holds to the testimony of Jesus? If so, then you must know that you are in a torrid, ferocious battle with Satan. Your enemy is continually spewing out rivers of sin and deception upon the world, but you can overcome him by having God's river of life flowing from within you! Jesus taught that a life built firmly on the Rock can withstand Satan's flood: "When a flood came, the torrent struck that house but could not shake it, because it was well built" (Luke 6:48).

God requires that His children live in the world but not be a part of the system that runs it. John wrote, "Do not love the world or anything in the world. If anyone loves the world, the love of the Father is not in him" (1 John 2:15). The only people in the world who are able to overcome the world system and not be contaminated by its filthy waters are those who personally know the Lord Jesus Christ. John encourages us later by explaining, "You, dear children, are from God and have overcome them, because the one who is in you is greater than the one who is in the world" (1 John 4:4).

God is able to completely protect His children and keep them safe and dry from the filthy water of the world, in much the same way the infant Moses was protected from harm as he floated down the River Nile. His mother coated the basket with pitch (Ex. 2:3), and the water did not touch him. God coats His children with righteousness, and we are able to be in the river yet not be affected by it as we progress through life.

In his great prayer to the Father, Jesus said, "I will remain in the world no longer, but they are still in the world, and I am coming to you. Holy Father, protect them by the power of your name – the name you gave me – so that they may be one as we are one. While I was with them, I protected them and kept them safe by that name you gave me. None has been lost except the one doomed to destruction so that Scripture would be fulfilled" (John 17:11–12).

When we live in the world yet refuse to submit to its rules and temptations, we will be different from those around us, and many will be attracted to us and our message. We will not only *have* a powerful witness; we will *be* a powerful witness. The Lord wants us to be "blameless and pure, children of God without fault in a crooked and depraved generation, in which you shine like stars in the universe as you hold out the word of life" (Phil. 2:15–16).

Have you been born again into God's kingdom? If so, you should know that "everyone born of God overcomes the world. This is the victory that has overcome the world, even our faith. Who is it that overcomes the world? Only he who believes that Jesus is the Son of God" (1 John 5:4–5).

During my first time in prison, I vividly remember that the

other men in my cell were completely bound with hopelessness. Most of them were hardened murderers and gangsters serving long prison sentences. Others were waiting to be executed. These men sang together each day, putting their own words to a popular tune. Part of their totally depressing song said, "The iron bars and prison walls have killed my dreams and hopes. I am locked inside this hopelessness, and all the beauty of the world outside has been taken away forever. I will never be free again."

When I heard these words, I felt grieved, and I created a new song for the men by changing the lyrics to their somber tune. They joined me in singing, "The iron bars and prison walls cannot keep the presence of God from me. He is with me every day. My surroundings cannot hinder God's love and presence, and because of Him I can live in a land of milk and honey."

Every one of my cellmates loved to sing this new song, and their hopelessness was gradually changed to hope as they opened their hearts to receive the Lord Jesus. This is one example of how a Christian can let the streams of living water flow into the lives of others.

God gave an extraordinary vision to Ezekiel. The prophet saw a river of life coming out of God's temple. He reported, "When it empties into the sea, the water there becomes fresh. Swarms of living creatures will live wherever the river flows. There will be large numbers of fish, because this water flows there and makes the salt water fresh; so where the river flows everything will live.... Fruit trees of all kinds will grow on both banks of the river. Their leaves will not wither, nor will their fruit fail. Every month they will bear, because the water from the sanctuary flows to them. Their fruit will serve for food and their leaves for healing" (Ezek. 47:8–9, 12).

What a wonderful vision Ezekiel had! These are the kinds of beautiful things that happen when God's living water starts to flow. Dry and dusty lives become fresh and alive again, and good fruit springs forth in the desert. In the Old Testament Ezekiel saw the water flowing from the temple in Jerusalem, but do you realize that today "you yourselves are God's temple and that God's Spirit lives in you? If anyone destroys God's temple, God will destroy him; for God's temple is sacred, and you are that temple" (1 Cor. 3:16–17).

This is such a wonderful truth. We need to get our minds off man-made temples, churches and buildings and realize that God no longer dwells in structures made by human hands. Paul told the Athenians, "The God who made the world and everything in it is the Lord of heaven and earth and does not live in temples built by hands" (Acts 17:24). He dwells inside those who believe in Jesus Christ!

I have seen God transform my country and have seen countless men and women, boys and girls experience streams of living water flowing out of them after the Holy Spirit came into their lives. I have seen hardened criminals and persecutors of the church fall to their knees like little children and repent of their sins as the Holy Spirit swept them into the kingdom of God. Brothers and sisters, I know that China will be saved! The river of life – which was once a dry creek in my country – has become a series of mighty waterways. Millions of people are being cleansed from their sin. This is why I have so much faith for the salvation of those parts of the world that currently seem, to the human mind, so difficult to reach with the gospel.

Muslims, Hindus and Buddhists are not beyond the cleansing power of God's mighty river of life! Atheists and terrorists will also see their lives transformed after they bathe in God's cleansing stream! For "there is a river whose streams make glad the city of God, the holy place where the Most High dwells" (Ps. 46:4).

More than a billion Muslims in the world today have yet to bathe in the streams of God's living water. Our Lord Jesus loves every one of them, and He longs to know them as His children. Nothing is more certain than He will bring out of these nations a powerful body of blood-bought Christians. I believe God is going to bring countless millions of Muslims into His kingdom before Jesus returns. God has not promised that the whole world will be full of sin, violence and unbelief. On the contrary, God's Word declares that "the earth will be filled with the knowledge of the glory of the LORD, as the waters cover the sea" (Hab. 2:14).

I know that many Christians find it hard to believe that a large number of Muslims will come to faith in Jesus Christ in these last days, but are Muslims any more difficult for God to reach than the Chinese were, or you were before you came to know Him? All the Muslims need is to taste and see the living water of God. Do you realize that the overwhelming majority of Muslims have never once heard the good news that Jesus came and died for them so that they can be free? If you had never heard the gospel in your entire life, would you be any better off than a Muslim today? It is only by the grace of God that anyone's life becomes transformed into the likeness of Jesus Christ. The apostle Paul posed a simple question: "How, then, can they call on the one they have not believed in? And how can they believe in the one of whom they have not heard? And how can they hear without someone preaching to them? And how can they preach unless they are sent?" (Rom. 10:14–15).

Instead of fearing and rejecting the Muslim world, we should love them, pray for them and do everything possible to reach them with the gospel. Don't give up on them, because Jesus certainly hasn't given up on the Muslims! In fact, He loves them deeply and longs for the day when they will be restored into right fellowship with Him and with all those descendants of Abraham who call on the name of the Lord. Let's not lose sight of the fact that many of the great figures in the Bible were once murderers and deceivers. The apostle Paul reminded the believers in Galatia, "For you have heard of my previous way of life in Judaism, how intensely I persecuted the church of God and tried to destroy it" (Gal. 1:13).

Aren't you glad that God didn't give up on Paul?

He raised him from the dead, figuratively speaking, and gave him a new life and purpose.

And aren't you glad God didn't give up on you? If you have been born again into God's kingdom, then you too have been raised from the dead, even though "once you were alienated from God and were enemies in your minds because of your evil behavior" (Col. 1:21). Paul reasons that "very rarely will anyone die for a righteous man, though for a good man someone might possibly dare to die. But God demonstrates his own love for us in this: While we were still sinners, Christ died for us" (Rom. 5:7–8).

God has long been turning contaminated water into living water. Before Elijah was taken to heaven in a whirlwind, Elisha asked for a double portion of his spirit. The very first miracle that Elisha performed occurred after the men of Jericho said to him, "Look, our lord, this town is well situated, as you can see, but the water is bad and the land is unproductive" (2 Kings 2:19).

Is this an accurate description of your own life, or your church? Is the water also bad and the land unproductive? If so, don't lose hope, because we serve a God who can intervene and transform your life. Elisha instructed the men to bring a new bowl with some salt in it. He threw the salt into the town's spring and declared, "This is what the LORD says: 'I have healed this water. Never again will it cause death or make the land unproductive.' And the water has remained wholesome to this day, according to the word Elisha had spoken" (2 Kings 2:21–22). When Jesus Christ changes you, not only will streams of living water flow from within, but that fresh blessing results in the surrounding land becoming productive.

Everywhere Jesus goes, streams of living water flow into the lives of people. He is the epitome of God's blessing and life. Wherever He is, the dead become alive and the barren become fruitful. Do you know that such is His power that when Jesus returns, the Bible states, "on that day his feet will stand on the Mount of Olives, east of Jerusalem, and the Mount of Olives will be split in two from east to west, forming a great valley, with half of the mountain moving north and half moving south.... On that day living water will flow out from Jerusalem, half to the eastern sea and half to the western sea, in summer and in winter. The LORD will be king over the whole earth. On that day there will be one LORD, and his name the only name" (Zech. 14:4, 8–9).

What a marvelous God we serve!

Now let me ask you something personal. Do you have streams of living water flowing from your life? Do you experience the joy of the Lord, or has your Christian life become dry and dusty, based on human intellect and empty rituals? Before you will ever see others experiencing God's living water, you will need to be immersed in it yourself.

If you have never experienced God's living water inside of you, then I encourage you to fall to your knees, cry out to God, and repent of your sins. Ask Him to change your life, and dedicate the rest of your days to serving God and not yourself.

If you do know God but it has been years since you felt that fresh presence of the Lord Jesus Christ in your life, then you too should fall to your knees and seek God. Remember both the warning and the promise that Jesus gave the church in Ephesus: "Remember the height from which you have fallen! Repent and do the things you did at first. If you do not repent, I will come to you and remove your lampstand from its place.... To him who overcomes, I will give the right to eat from the tree of life, which is in the paradise of God" (Rev. 2:5, 7).

God – who loves you so much that He pursued you until you became one of His children – desires to have an intimate and life-giving relationship with you. I invite you right now to open your heart and accept Jesus Christ as your personal Savior. To all who believe in His Son, God gives His grace and provides living water to flow from within you, bringing life to every area of your life that has been unfruitful and broken.

13

Hearing God's Voice

"The sheep listen to his voice. He calls his own sheep by name and leads them out. When he has brought out all his own, he goes on ahead of them, and his sheep follow him because they know his voice. But they will never follow a stranger; in fact, they will run away from him because they do not recognize a stranger's voice."

John 10:3–5

 Jesus said His sheep listen to His voice and the Good Shepherd recognizes and calls each one by name. In Jesus, I have a simple theology. I believe God speaks to His children all the time. We just need to listen and obey. When we start to obey His voice, we see God's power and authority in us and operating through us.

Of course the main way that God speaks to His sheep is through the Bible. Nothing God says will contradict the Scriptures, nor will He ever add to them or take away from them. But I also believe that the Holy Spirit guides followers of Christ by directing and guiding them daily. We see this happening in the book of Acts. On one occasion the apostle Paul was "kept by the Holy Spirit from preaching the word in the province of Asia" (Acts 16:6), only to then receive a vision of a man from Macedonia begging him to come and help (Acts 16:9). On another occasion Paul proclaimed, "And now, compelled by the Spirit, I am going to Jerusalem, not knowing what will happen to me there. I only know that in every city the Holy Spirit warns me that prison and hardships are facing me" (Acts 20:22–23).

How was it that the Holy Spirit directed, compelled and warned Paul? Was it solely a result of his reading the Scriptures? Surely Paul was in constant fellowship with the Father and heard His voice guiding him along the way. Isaiah prophesied that a day would come when the people of God would be guided by His voice: "Whether you turn to the right or to the left, your ears will hear a voice behind you, saying, 'This is the way; walk in it'" (Isa. 30:21).

On numerous occasions, preachers in China have traveled to a remote mountainous area to visit a group of believers. Although nobody is told that they are coming, when the preachers arrive they often find the believers already gathered together and expecting them, sometimes even in the middle of the night! When asked how they knew the preachers were coming at that time, they reply, "The Lord told us to get ready because you were coming at this time."

In other places, the house churches had problems when undercover agents came along to spy on the believers and see if they could gather information that might be used against them later. The Christians prayed and asked God what they should do. The Lord told them to stop announcing the place and time of their meetings and instead just trust that the Holy Spirit would reveal the details to each person He wanted to come to the meeting.

On the day of the next meeting, nobody except the leader knew where the church service would be held, or at what time, but one by one believers began to turn up, all having been told where to go while they were praying earlier that morning. This method is one way of making sure that only those people the Lord wants to fellowship together actually do so. It also put an immediate end to the unwanted visits by the undercover agents.

The Bible is full of examples of God's people hearing and following His voice. Listening is an integral part of having a relationship with someone. Can you imagine what kind of marriage it would be if a husband and wife never heard one another's voice? So it is for a child of God who has a relationship with the Father.

I am convinced that one of the reasons many Christians struggle to hear God's voice is simply because they don't take time to be quiet and listen. Their lives are so busy with irrelevant things that they go months at a time without ever stopping and quieting their hearts before the Lord. To hear God's voice, you have to stop listening to your own heart and mind. You need to stop listening to the news and to people who love to air their worthless opinions. You also need to stop taking heed of the voice of Satan and giving attention to evil thoughts. Jesus told us, "When you pray, go into your room, close the door and pray to your Father, who is unseen. Then your Father, who sees what is done in secret, will reward you. And when you pray, do not keep on babbling like pagans, for they think they will be heard because of their many words. Do not be like them, for your Father knows what you need before you ask him" (Matt. 6:6–8).

Those engaged in ministry for the Lord can easily get sidetracked so that they spend little or no time quietly listening to Him. Throughout the Bible we are encouraged to "be still, and know that I am God" (Ps. 46:10). Elijah had a remarkable experience that reveals much about the nature of God and the requirements for those who desire to hear His voice. Elijah was hiding in a cave on Mount Horeb when God told him to stand on the mountain because He was about to pass by. First, "a great and powerful wind tore the mountains apart and shattered the rocks before the LORD, but the LORD was not in the wind. After the wind there was an earthquake, but the LORD was not in the earthquake. After the earthquake came a fire, but the LORD was not in the fire. And after the fire came a gentle whisper. When Elijah heard it, he pulled his cloak over his face and went out and stood at the mouth of the cave. Then a voice said to him, 'What are you doing here, Elijah?'" (1 Kings 19:11–13).

Brothers and sisters, God does not often shout. If the world is making a lot of noise, God does not make Himself heard by speaking even louder than it. Rather, He speaks in a whisper, and only those who are willing to get away from the roar of the world will be able to hear Him speak.

Another important thing every follower of Jesus must learn is that God's methods and strategies are never exactly the same in any two situations. It is futile to use a strategy God gave a hundred years ago, or last year, or even last week. He is not some kind of machine. He is a personal, intimate God, and His mercies are new every morning! After the Israelites crossed the Red Sea, they were led by a pillar of cloud by day and a pillar of fire at night. The children of Israel had to follow the Lord whenever the cloud or fire moved. If they were too slow, they would be left behind. We must hear His voice and receive His guidance every day. When we do so, we will be amazed at the number of opportunities that open for us to share His love with people.

It's hard for a person with the fear of man to properly hear God's voice, because he will always be worried about the different opinions and criticisms people have. They will prevent you from moving forward and fulfilling all that God has for you to do. That is why the Bible says, "Fear of man will prove to be a snare" (Prov. 29:25). On the other hand, "He who fears the LORD has a secure fortress, and for his children it will be a refuge. The fear of the LORD is a fountain of life, turning a man from the snares of death" (Prov. 14:26–27).

The world cannot stop a child of God who follows God and walks in obedience to His commands. We need to throw off the fear of man and steadfastly decide to live only for Jesus. We have no right to be afraid of what people think or say about us. In fact, we have no right to even be interested in people's opinions of us. We are meant to be dead to this world and everything that it represents. A dead person doesn't care what he looks like or what others think of him. All that matters is God! For "he is before all things, and in him all things hold together. And he is the head of the body, the church; he is the beginning and the firstborn from among the dead, so that in everything he might have the supremacy" (Col. 1:17–18).

From what I have seen, many Christians think that the only place a Christian can hear the voice of the Lord is during church services on Sunday mornings. This time is often set aside for "spiritual" purposes, and the rest of the week is set aside for "secular" pursuits. Such a separation is completely unbiblical and a corrosive influence in your life. It's not enough just to attend church and listen to teaching. God requires you to take that teaching and live it among the community during the week. How else will the lost people around you be saved?

Jesus said His disciples are the light of the world and the salt of the earth. The darker a place is, the more lights it needs. The more rotten a place has become, the more salt it needs. Wherever true Christians are found, even among flavorless communities, the pleasant aroma of Jesus Christ will be present. "For we are to God the aroma of Christ among those who are being saved and those who are perishing. To the one we are the smell of death; to the other, the fragrance of life" (2 Cor. 2:15–16).

It is dangerous to be the kind of Christian who listens to biblical teaching but does not go out and live what they have been taught. The Bible says such a person is "deceived." James warns us, "Do not merely listen to the word, and so deceive yourselves. Do what it says. Anyone who listens to the word but does not do what it says is like a man who looks at his face in a mirror and, after looking at himself, goes away and immediately forgets what he looks like. But the man who looks intently into the perfect law that gives freedom, and continues to do this, not forgetting what he has heard, but doing it – he will be blessed in what he does" (James 1:22–25).

It is time for more Christians to be like Augustine, who would read the Gospels in the morning and then go out in the afternoon and put into action what he had just read. When Augustine read about the rich young ruler, he went and gave his possessions to the poor. When he read how Jesus washed the feet of His disciples, Augustine washed the feet of his brothers in Christ.

God works through people who are willing to obey His Word. The Lord has declared, "This is the one I esteem: he who is humble and contrite in spirit, and trembles at my word" (Isa. 66:2). Don't think that it is too hard to obey God's commands. If you feel this way, then you are confused. Perhaps you have been so pressured to obey human traditions and requirements that you have confused God's commands with those of men. The Bible says, "This is how we know that we love the children of God: by loving God and carrying out his commands. This is love for God: to obey his commands. And his commands are not burdensome, for everyone born of God overcomes the world. This is the victory that has overcome the world, even our faith" (1 John 5:2–4).

We must block our ears to all other voices that vie for our attention and determine only to listen and obey the voice of the Holy Spirit. Many times, Christians hear the voices of past failures and successes, and the deafening voice of church tradition rings in their ears. The temptation is to let these voices cause us to think that what God has done in the past He will do today. But this is not necessarily true. God never changes, but the strategies He gives to His children to help them reach the generation in which they live constantly change. We need the ability to hear the voice of God and the sensitivity to discern what God is doing today.

When you start to obey God and give your life unreservedly to His purposes, He will begin to share His heart with you. This is surely the greatest privilege, apart from salvation, that any person can experience on this earth! When God shares His heart with you, you will have a new understanding of His love, for "if anyone acknowledges that Jesus is the Son of God, God lives in him and he in God. And so we know and rely on the love God has for us. God is love. Whoever lives in love lives in God, and God in him" (1 John 4:15–16).

The heart of God beats for all the nations of the world and for each individual created in His image. He passionately loves each man and woman, boy and girl. His heart is bursting with love and compassion. He longs for everyone to be saved, "not wanting anyone to perish, but everyone to come to repentance" (2 Peter 3:9).

Not only does God love the whole world, but He loves you! He wants to show you His glory in Jesus Christ and to use you for His kingdom on this earth.

14

True Unity

> How good and pleasant it is
>> when brothers live together in unity!
> It is like precious oil poured on the head,
>> running down on the beard,
> running down on Aaron's beard,
>> down upon the collar of his robes.
> It is as if the dew of Hermon
>> were falling on Mount Zion.
> For there the LORD bestows his blessing,
>> even life forevermore.

Psalm 133:1–3

It is natural for us to love the places where we are born and grow up. Jesus loved Bethlehem and Galilee, and the Gospels record that He wept over Jerusalem, because the city had rejected His love and His teaching. After He was told that Herod wanted to kill him, Jesus cried out, "O Jerusalem, Jerusalem, you who kill the prophets and stone those sent to you, how often I have longed to gather your children together, as a hen gathers her chicks under her wings, but you were not willing! Look, your house is left to you desolate. I tell you, you will not see me again until you say, 'Blessed is he who comes in the name of the Lord' " (Luke 13:34–35).

During the three and a half years Jesus spent with His disciples, He constantly tried to bring unity among them so that they would learn to love one another and not try to put themselves first. This proved difficult to do, for their ears were dim and their minds were slow to understand the purposes of God.

Even up until the time of Jesus' death and resurrection, the disciples did not understand that God's plan was for His Son to bleed and die for the sins of the world. Their understanding was dulled because of their pride and selfish ambition. Jesus told the disciples, " 'Listen carefully to what I am about to tell you: The Son of Man is going to be betrayed into the hands of men.' But they did not understand what this meant. It was hidden from them, so that they did not grasp it, and they were afraid to ask him about it" (Luke 9:44–45).

Jesus had just plainly told his followers that He would suffer persecution, but the very next verse tells us that "an argument started among the disciples as to which of them would be the greatest. Jesus, knowing their thoughts, took a little child and had him stand beside him. Then he said to them, 'Whoever welcomes this little child in my name welcomes me; and whoever welcomes me welcomes the one who sent me. For he who is least among you all—he is the greatest' " (Luke 9:46–48).

In addition, the apostle Paul taught that we should "do nothing out of selfish ambition or vain conceit, but in humility consider others better than yourselves. Each of you should look not only to your own interests, but also to the interests of others" (Phil. 2:3–4). Unity will never be achieved unless this kind of humility exists among the children of God.

After their Master was painfully crucified and killed, the

disciples made their way to Galilee, for that was their home. When disaster strikes and our world is turned upside down, we tend to go back home so we can be in familiar surroundings. The disciples, who were now eleven in number, went to the mountain where Jesus had instructed them to go, and the resurrected Lord appeared to them. Jesus didn't waste any time. He got right to the point, and the first thing He said was, "All authority in heaven and on earth has been given to me. Therefore go and make disciples of all nations, baptizing them in the name of the Father and of the Son and of the Holy Spirit, and teaching them to obey everything I have commanded you. And surely I am with you always, to the very end of the age" (Matt. 28:18–20).

This is the solution to true Christian unity!

Most of our church disputes and petty infighting come when we start arguing about unimportant matters. Our eyes come off the Great Commission and we start to fight one another instead of fighting against the works of the Devil, which is the very reason Jesus Christ came into the world. The Bible plainly declares, "The reason the Son of God appeared was to destroy the devil's work" (1 John 3:8).

So often Christians believe they have to arrive at complete doctrinal unity before they can work together. This is unlikely to occur. Doctrine, of course, is incredibly important, but I have never met two Christians who believe exactly the same about every issue in the Bible. We must agree with other Christians on the major foundational doctrines of the Bible, such as those the writer of Hebrews lists: "Therefore let us leave the elementary teachings about Christ and go on to maturity, not laying again the foundation of repentance from acts that lead to death, and of faith in God, instruction about baptisms, the laying on of hands, the resurrection of the dead, and eternal judgment. And God permitting, we will do so" (Heb. 6:1–3).

Many Christians seem to be good at sitting around trying to perfect their doctrine, but few seem to obey Jesus' command to go into the world and make disciples of all nations. We need to stop trying to play games with God. Many believers want people to think they are pious, when in reality they are living in disobedience and deception.

In China I was involved for many years with trying to bring unity among the various branches of the house churches. This was one of the most difficult things I have ever been called to do.

For most of the 1980s, the house churches in China were unified. We all served Jesus together and didn't care what kind of group we belonged to. We all belonged to Jesus, and that was all that mattered.

Things started to change in the late 1980s and early 1990s. Many Western Christians had heard about the tremendous revival going on in China, and they wanted to be a part of it. They sent representatives to China to meet with house church leaders. They told us we weren't educated enough and that our greatest need was for more theological training. They assured us, "Our denomination has the best training program. We will bless you with it." For years believers had come to Hong Kong and carried Bibles across the border to us in China, and we were very grateful. Now, however, thousands of teaching books were also being carried across, promoting certain favorite doctrines of each denomination.

Before this happened, things had been much simpler. Jesus was our teacher and professor. We didn't ask one another what school we had attended. Rather, we asked, "In which prison have you been receiving your higher education from the Lord?"

When I was in prison in 1991, some close brothers came to visit me. With tears in their eyes, they reported what was going on in the church and said that Satan was reconstructing barriers between God's children. These were the same barriers the Lord had just spent thirty years dismantling so that His living water would flow freely and without hindrance throughout His church!

After I was released from prison, I recommenced preaching the gospel. Things were different, however, and everywhere I went I was asked, "Brother, what church do you belong to?" I replied, "I just belong to Jesus. I am called to be a witness for Jesus." This answer did not satisfy those who asked me.

My heart was pierced by these developments, and I was grieved to see the walls being erected to divide God's children. I cried out in prayer, "Lord Jesus, China does not need all these teachings and denominations. China needs You!"

Tragically, there are still Western denominations and ministries today that are trying to erect barriers between China's Christians. They did not come to China just to serve the body of Christ, but rather to impose their own beliefs and agendas on us. This is a tragic and bitter blow for the kingdom of God. Many organizations claim they exist to serve the Chinese church, but in reality, the way they function gives the appearance that they think Chinese Christians exist only to serve their agendas.

I came to realize that some of the doctrinal beliefs or styles of worship between the different groups meant we would never arrive at complete doctrinal unity, at least not until Jesus returns. However, it was clear we agreed on the fundamental doctrines of the Bible, and we realized we needed to cooperate and put aside our own ways of doing things in order to fulfill the Great Commission.

The main area in which Christians in China are able to find unity is in the work of God. We realize that even though we express our faith in a variety of different ways, we are all called to preach the gospel with one mind and to extend the kingdom of God with one heart. Many of the house churches focus on different forms of ministry, but we realize we need to unite with one another and love one another as different members of the same family of God.

We humbled ourselves and asked God to help us prioritize those things that are most important to Him. I believe the most important thing for the church to do is to proclaim the gospel throughout the whole world, to every nation. The Devil is an expert at getting us distracted from this. He doesn't mind our doing all kinds of different Christian activities, as long as we don't get busy reaching lost, hell-bound nations for Jesus Christ.

In China the church has seen 100,000,000 people transformed by the power and love of Jesus Christ. And it is only just the start. In many ways it has been just like the book of Acts, and God has been with us as we have put aside our petty squabbles and gone forth proclaiming the truth.

My friend, do not sit around waiting to become perfect before you feel qualified to serve God. That day will never come in your lifetime! Go forth and do what Jesus commanded all of His followers to do, and the Lord will change your life as you obey Him. In one of his least-known epistles, the apostle Paul wrote, "I pray that you may be active in sharing your faith, so that you will have a full understanding of every good thing we have in Christ" (Philem. 6). It is only when you share your faith and obey God's Word that you begin to experience the fullness of God's blessings and presence flowing through your life. This is a principle that many Christians have sadly missed. We need to take our eyes off ourselves and start serving God! This is also the greatest remedy for selfishness. In numerous places the Bible contrasts the different consequences between those who look outward and give away what they have, and those who hold on to their blessings. For example, Proverbs 11:24–26 says:

> *One man gives freely, yet gains even more;*
> *another withholds unduly, but comes to poverty.*
> *A generous man will prosper;*
> *he who refreshes others will himself be refreshed.*
> *People curse the man who hoards grain,*
> *but blessing crowns him who is willing to sell.*

We have been given a great blessing, salvation by Jesus Christ, but we have also been given the responsibility to spread it as far and wide as possible during our lifetime. Jesus warned us with parables about those who keep the light to themselves rather than share it around. If you are a child of God, don't ignore the stern warning Jesus gave His disciples: "That servant who knows his master's will and does not get ready or does not do what his master wants will be beaten with many blows. But the one who does not know and does things deserving punishment will be beaten with few blows. From everyone who has been given much, much will be demanded; and from the one who has been entrusted with much, much more will be asked" (Luke 12:47–48).

Dear friends, let's humble ourselves and call on the Lord

to make us into usable vessels, one God can use for His glory among the nations. Let's cry out to the King of Kings, asking forgiveness for our pride, begging Him to release us from deception and the sin of disobedience.

Then, as we rise from our knees, let us ask our heavenly Father to open our eyes and help us see what is important to Him. Ask the Holy Spirit to show you the harvest fields of the world! It is time for us to stop our posturing and to stop making excuses for our disobedience. Jesus said, "Do you not say, 'Four months more and then the harvest'? I tell you, open your eyes and look at the fields! They are ripe for harvest" (John 4:35).

15

The God of Power

Great is the LORD and most worthy of praise;
his greatness no one can fathom.
One generation will commend your works to another;
they will tell of your mighty acts.
They will speak of the glorious splendor of your majesty,
and I will meditate on your wonderful works.
They will tell of the power of your awesome works,
and I will proclaim your great deeds.

Psalm 145:3–6

*O*ur God is the almighty God. It must have been incredible to be in Jerusalem in those precious days between the
resurrection of the Lord Jesus Christ and His return to heaven.
During this time the apostle Paul records that "he appeared
to more than five hundred of the brothers at the same time"
(1 Cor. 15:6).

Can you imagine what it was like in those days? Remember
that at the precise moment Jesus died, "the earth shook and the
rocks split. The tombs broke open and the bodies of many holy
people who had died were raised to life. They came out of the

tombs, and after Jesus' resurrection they went into the holy city and appeared to many people" (Matt. 27:51–53).

Now this must have been some sight to behold! I wonder how Herod, Pilate, the scribes and Pharisees and all the enemies of Jesus dealt with the sudden appearance of all these holy people who had risen from their tombs!

The disciples spent some extraordinary times with Jesus after the resurrection. On one occasion they shared a meal together, and Jesus commanded them, "Do not leave Jerusalem, but wait for the gift my Father promised, which you have heard me speak about. For John baptized with water, but in a few days you will be baptized with the Holy Spirit" (Acts 1:4–5).

The disciples didn't understand what Jesus meant, and they asked if He was about to restore a political kingdom to Israel, to bring them out from under the control of the cruel Romans. Jesus replied, " 'It is not for you to know the times or dates the Father has set by his own authority. But you will receive power when the Holy Spirit comes on you; and you will be my witnesses in Jerusalem, and in all Judea and Samaria, and to the ends of the earth.' After he said this, he was taken up before their very eyes, and a cloud hid him from their sight" (Acts 1:7–9).

One hundred twenty disciples gathered together in the upper room in Jerusalem, praying to God and waiting for the gift that Jesus had promised. After they were baptized with the Holy Spirit, the lives of these disciples were dramatically altered forever. Peter was transformed from a man who denied Christ three times to a powerful evangelist. Three thousand people were saved on the day of Pentecost after Peter stood up and proclaimed the way of salvation.

The other apostles also experienced a dramatic transformation in their lives. Those who had deserted Jesus at the time of His greatest need ended up being such bold witnesses of the Truth after being endued with the power of the Holy Spirit that they were martyred for their faith. The book of Acts records how the fire of the gospel spread throughout the Roman world, to Rome itself and to many areas along the Mediterranean coast. A short time later, the Jews said of Paul and Silas, "These men who have caused trouble all over the world have now come here" (Acts 17:6).

In the years I served God in China, I was privileged to see many instances of God's power operating through His church. I have witnessed countless people dramatically healed from illnesses, including cancer and leprosy. Once during a meeting when the power of God was present, a nearby mental hospital brought about a dozen of their patients, and all of them were completely healed after coming into contact with Jesus Christ. Their sanity was restored and they were subsequently discharged from the hospital.

In 1997 I reached my lowest point when I was imprisoned because of the testimony of Jesus, and my legs were crushed so that I could not walk. It was my darkest hour, and many house church leaders were also arrested and thrown into prison. My wife was incarcerated in the women's prison.

God commanded me to get up and walk out of the prison, and by His great power He made the way for me to escape. Many brothers and sisters in China have experienced similar things in their lives and ministries while serving the Lord. In all these things, however, the greatest miracle we have seen occurs whenever a sinner repents and believes in Jesus Christ. The resultant new life is always astonishing to observe. All around the world our loving King is saving and cleansing multitudes of people from every tribe, language, people and nation. Only our almighty God can say, "I will sprinkle clean water on you, and you will be clean; I will cleanse you from all your impurities and from all your idols. I will give you a new heart and put a new spirit in you; I will remove from you your heart of stone and give you a heart of flesh. And I will put my Spirit in you and move you to follow my decrees and be careful to keep my laws" (Ezek. 36:25–27).

After I arrived in the West, it didn't take long for me to realize that something fundamental was missing in the body of Christ. That missing thing was the power and presence of God. I don't say this to condemn anyone, but rather I point it out in the hope that it will speak to your heart and help the church. Thousands of churches today do not preach the Word with the authority and power that Jesus promised to all who follow Him. This is a tragedy, as such powerless churches end up relying on human wisdom to see "results." The fruit of such a half-baked gospel invariably produces a harvest of half-baked believers, most of whom will fall away at the first sign of trouble.

Countless churches, missions and families are full of deadness. This is a terrible stain on the name of the Lord Jesus Christ, who is the living God. Everything He does produces abundant life. Jesus said that Satan "comes only to steal and kill and destroy; I have come that they may have life, and have it to the full" (John 10:10). Jesus never attended a funeral where the person remained dead. The same applies today. If He turns up, our homes and churches will be dramatically changed.

The good news is that Jesus has not changed! All our human methods and techniques will result in failure and amount to nothing if God is not with us in His power and glory. When

Jesus comes in, He breaks off the shackles and people's lives are instantly transformed. You never have to look for help from big-name preachers when the glory of God is present! It is all about God, not man. One second in the presence of God's glory can achieve more than years of human endeavor!

These days there are many preachers who have attended seminary and learned how to speak in public, but if that is all they have, you will do well not to listen to their messages. If the words being preached are empowered by mere human wisdom, they will not benefit the listeners in any spiritual way. The apostle Paul was a very smart, highly educated man. Yet he was careful not to rely on those attributes when he shared God's Word. Pay careful attention to what he told the Corinthians: "My message and my preaching were not with wise and persuasive words, but with a demonstration of the Spirit's power, so that your faith might not rest on men's wisdom, but on God's power" (1 Cor. 2:4–5).

Did you know that it is possible for your faith to rest in the wrong place? Paul wanted the Corinthians' faith to rest on God's power and not on the wisdom of this world. When this sound advice is followed, it produces strong followers of Christ who will not fall away when tested. In China most people come to Christ after they see a demonstration of the power of God. Perhaps they are healed from an illness or set free from oppression. After people experience the power and authority of God for themselves, they have no trouble believing the gospel and giving their lives to Christ. Not to do so would be to deny the reality of their experiences.

We want to take the gospel into the Muslim world. There are more than one billion captives to Satan among the Islamic nations. Jesus has already paid the price for their salvation, and

He will not rest until He takes possession of what is rightfully His. He loves them dearly.

If you go to reach Muslims, it is not enough just to take the Bible in your hands and argue with them. They will meet you with the Qur'an held aloft and tell you, "We already have the Holy Scriptures!" The only way to reach Muslims for Jesus is for them to experience the living water of the Holy Spirit flowing into their lives. They do not need dialogue or theological forums. They need a personal encounter with the living God! It is easy for Muslims to argue with you about the merits of Christianity until they are blue in the face, but when they personally experience the power and grace of Jesus Christ in their lives, all arguments cease and they need no more persuading that He is indeed the risen Lord.

Do you believe that God can work through you in such a way? Can He use you to do miracles so that Jesus Christ may be glorified and many people experience salvation? The apostle Paul issued a challenge to some of the believers in Corinth: "I will come to you very soon, if the Lord is willing, and then I will find out not only how these arrogant people are talking, but what power they have. For the kingdom of God is not a matter of talk but of power" (1 Cor. 4:19–20).

Satan wants people to think that the sustenance they need to live a successful life can be found inside themselves or in the things surrounding them. They search for substitutes in a bid to procure the true joy and peace that only come by knowing Jesus Christ. The moment people fall for the lie that they can prosper without God, they cut themselves off from His presence and power, for "the mind of sinful man is death, but the mind controlled by the Spirit is life and peace; the sinful mind is hostile to God. It does not submit to God's law, nor can it do so. Those controlled by the sinful nature cannot please God" (Rom. 8:6–8).

During the times of strongest revival in China, miracles were so commonplace that we didn't even think about them much. They were as natural as breathing the air. They helped thrust millions of people into the kingdom of God and strengthened the faith of all who experienced such miracles. Even young children went out and shared the gospel with other children, and mighty miracles of healing, deliverance and signs and wonders accompanied them wherever they went. This was not considered strange, because the Lord Jesus promised us, "Whoever believes and is baptized will be saved, but whoever does not believe will be condemned. And these signs will accompany those who believe: In my name they will drive out demons; they will speak in new tongues; they will pick up snakes with their hands; and when they drink deadly poison, it will not hurt them at all; they will place their hands on sick people, and they will get well" (Mark 16:16–18).

When you present the gospel to somebody, it needs to come with a demonstration of the power of the Holy Spirit. This may occur in a variety of different ways, such as through a healing, or a word of knowledge about a person's life, or the working of another gift. The demonstration of God's power convinces unbelievers that the message is true and that Jesus is alive today! When the power of the gospel is truly demonstrated, only the most hard-hearted of people are unwilling to respond to the claims of Christ upon their lives.

Miracles and signs and wonders are not just for within the walls of your church building. No! They are to be demonstrated among the people, in the marketplace, on the bustling city streets, and in the homes of those who are trapped in darkness.

This is where Jesus and the disciples did most of their miracles. They knew nothing about scheduled "healing meetings" inside church buildings. The power of God accompanied them wherever they proclaimed the good news that the kingdom of God is available to all who put their trust in Jesus Christ.

Christianity without the power of God is no Christianity at all! Power is a fundamental part of God's workings with humankind throughout history. On every page of the Bible, you can read about God's miraculous power in operation, beginning with the very first verse of the Bible, when "God created the heavens and the earth." It continues throughout the Old and New Testaments, right up to the conclusion of the book of Revelation when Jesus declares, "I am the Alpha and the Omega, the First and the Last, the Beginning and the End" (Rev. 22:13).

Did you ever ponder that God is so powerful He didn't even need to create the universe with His hands? He simply spoke, and it came into existence. Our God is not just mighty. He is all-mighty. He is not only powerful. He is all-powerful. In speaking of the majesty of our Lord, the Bible records that "earth and sky fled from his presence, and there was no place for them" (Rev. 20:11). His power is beyond compare!

What kind of message does your church preach?

Is your faith based on men's wisdom or on God's power? The Bible warns us that in the last days there will be some people "having a form of godliness but denying its power. Have nothing to do with them" (2 Tim. 3:5).

Many Christians have developed a very warped view of God. They think He only works the way they want Him to, according to their own plans. Such thinking is terribly sad and dangerous. God can never be limited. He is God! When we lose a proper perspective on God's power and love, we harm ourselves and those around us. Such limited thinking becomes like a cancer, devouring our spiritual life and bringing death where God intends for there to be life.

If you are a Christian, I encourage you to examine your heart and ask God to reveal those areas of your life where you have placed limits on Him.

You may know in your head that God is powerful, but have you allowed Him to use His power to break you free from the prison of sinful habits and attitudes?

You may know in your head that Jesus said, "All authority in heaven and on earth has been given to me" (Matt. 28:18), but do you ever pray in faith for someone to be healed or to be delivered from demons?

You may know in your head that the historical Jesus is powerful, but do you realize that He wants to share His power with you so that you can be His ambassador to a lost and hurting world?

The time is short, and God is looking for people who are serious about His kingdom. He wants to empower you to walk in purity and to proclaim the gospel throughout the earth.

If you are a follower of Jesus Christ, it's time to wake up and stop living in a weak and pale way that denies the power of God. Repent from such a narrow, impoverished view of our Lord, and ask Jesus to reveal His power in your life.

If you are a pastor or church leader, I encourage you not to get in the way of what God wants to do among His people. He alone is the Shepherd, and He is jealous for His beloved flock. Do not continue to expend energy trying to squeeze God into your narrow theological box. Submit your life afresh to Him, and allow Him to have His way among His people. It's time for change! It's time for the church to throw off the stench of death and once again become alive, as Jesus is alive! As you draw near to Him, He will draw near to you, and you will begin to experience His power and authority in your life.

16

Fishing Lessons

> Simon Peter climbed aboard and dragged the net
> ashore. It was full of large fish, 153, but even with so many
> the net was not torn.
>
> *John 21:11*

The Word of God is full of encouragement and lessons for those with teachable hearts and ears to hear what the Holy Spirit is saying to them. If you follow and obey the Word of God, you will not only see miracles; your life will become a working miracle.

When Jesus first called Peter, James and John to follow Him, He found them working on their fishing boats down at the shore of the Sea of Galilee. It is interesting to note that Jesus didn't just look for those who were interested in fishing; He chose those who were professional fishermen. Similarly, Jesus today knows those Christians who are serious about catching fish for the kingdom of God, not those who merely show an interest in the results without a willingness to commit to the process.

Peter, James and John were cleaning their nets when the King of Kings approached them, climbed into one of their boats and asked to be taken out a little way from shore so He could teach the people. The Bible doesn't record what Jesus taught that day, but when He was finished, he told Simon Peter, "Put out into deep water, and let down the nets for a catch" (Luke 5:4).

This initial contact with Jesus completely altered the course of Peter, John and James's lives. All three became His disciples and saw and did things they could never have imagined. Jesus called them that day, and despite their weaknesses and failings, He never took that calling away, "for God's gifts and his call are irrevocable" (Rom. 11:29). This is wonderful news for you and me! God does not change His mind. When He calls someone, He will never abandon them, for "God has said, 'Never will I leave you; never will I forsake you'" (Heb. 13:5).

In the world, people abandon one another all the time and barely think twice about it. Not so with God. The Bible even says, "If we are faithless, he will remain faithful, for he cannot disown himself" (2 Tim. 2:13). When God commits to a project, He always completes it. The good news is that we, His children, are His most treasured projects of all. Paul wrote that we should be "confident of this, that he who began a good work in you will carry it on to completion until the day of Christ Jesus" (Phil. 1:6).

Perhaps you have been following Jesus for a number of years and have lost touch with His plan for your life. If that is so, then repent on your knees and ask God to forgive and cleanse you. Then ask the Holy Spirit to put your life back on the right path that God called you to walk on. Even if you have been disobedient and rebellious to the Lord, He is able to transform your life and "repay you for the years the locusts have eaten" (Joel 2:25).

Now when Jesus told Peter to take his boat back out onto the Sea of Galilee, Peter no doubt was taken aback. After all, he was the experienced fisherman. He had probably heard that Jesus was a carpenter from the landlocked town of Nazareth. Peter no doubt thought it was a stupid idea to go fishing in the daylight, as everyone knows that fish stay away from the bright surface during the day. Yet something deep inside Peter told him to put aside all of these misgivings and do what Jesus was telling him to do. Even though it went against all human logic, Peter answered, "Master, we've worked hard all night and haven't caught anything. But because you say so, I will let down the nets" (Luke 5:5).

It always pays to obey Jesus! He knows what is best for your life, even when it doesn't seem to make logical sense at the time. This passage shows us that Peter possessed a simple faith underneath his rough exterior. His rugged and confrontational personality got him into trouble plenty of times, but his childlike faith and obedience also thrilled the heart of Jesus. Many preachers have mocked Peter for his attempt to walk on the water when Jesus called him, but they fail to mention that none of the other disciples even had the faith to get out of the boat! And let's not forget that for a few seconds Peter *did* walk on water.

All of the most memorable experiences in my own life have come when Jesus told me to do something that seemed completely contrary to the circumstances around me. This was certainly the case when He told me to walk out of the Zhengzhou Prison in 1997. I clearly heard Jesus' voice command me to stand up and go. For a few moments I struggled with this command, and my mind began to apply human reason to the situation

Then another strong and clear voice spoke to my heart, saying, "This prison is real, but I am the Truth!"

I obeyed, and the Lord blinded the eyes of many guards and opened prison doors for me to escape. Through this wonderful experience I learned an important lesson about obedience. God does not expect us to argue with Him when He tells us to do something. He doesn't expect us to apply human logic to our circumstances. He simply expects us to obey and trust Him. I have found that whenever we step out in obedience to God's voice, miracles follow. If you trust in God's Word, you will never regret it. Obedience allows you to operate despite seemingly impossible circumstances, because Jesus is more powerful than everything we can see or touch. It is written, "By faith we understand that the universe was formed at God's command, so that what is seen was not made out of what was visible" (Heb. 11:3).

On countless occasions house church believers in China have been alerted by the Holy Spirit to immediately leave a meeting place. It made no sense to do so at the time, but they obeyed and fled, only for the police to turn up moments later to find an empty meeting room!

Peter, John and James also did what the Lord told them, and "when they had done so, they caught such a large number of fish that their nets began to break. So they signaled their partners in the other boat to come and help them, and they came and filled both boats so full that they began to sink" (Luke 5:6–7).

When Jesus does something remarkable in our lives, our initial reaction is often one of deep awareness of our own sinfulness and shortcomings. Peter "fell at Jesus' knees and said, 'Go away from me, Lord; I am a sinful man!' For he and all his companions were astonished at the catch of fish they had taken, and so were James and John, the sons of Zebedee, Simon's partners" (Luke 5:8–10).

What a day Peter had! Just hours earlier he had spent a whole night sitting in his boat without catching a single fish. After he met Jesus, his life was completely transformed and given new purpose and direction. Jesus said to Peter, " 'Don't be afraid; from now on you will catch men.' So they pulled their boats up on shore, left everything and followed him" (Luke 5:10–11).

We need to realize that when God speaks to us, He is always right. He is not like a person who gets some things right and other things wrong. He is right 100 percent of the time, and we should trust Him 100 percent of the time. The very first words ever spoken in this universe were the words of our Lord, when He created the earth and everything in it.

Let me ask you a question. Where were the fish when Peter was trying to catch them all night?

They were right there in the darkness of the water, unseen by Peter and his companions. They easily avoided the nets set for them. But the next morning Jesus, the Creator of the world, knew exactly where each fish was. He made each one of them. Imagine how excited those little fish must have been to hear the voice of their Creator. Maybe they came closer to the surface to catch a glimpse of the Lord of heaven and gladly swam over to Peter's boat and climbed into his nets, just so they could have the privilege of obeying the almighty Son of God! Did you know that all of God's creation "waits in eager expectation for the sons of God to be revealed" (Rom. 8:19)?

In China we have seen the hardest sinners fall to their knees in repentance when they came face-to-face with Jesus. We have seen numerous murderers, rapists and prostitutes caught up in God's net because they heard the voice of Jesus calling them.

On a later occasion the disciples heard Jesus say, "Let us go over to the other side." They then made their way out onto the lake, taking "him along, just as he was, in the boat" (Mark 4:35–36). Jesus was soon asleep, and a fierce storm arose.

As you launch into your ministry, make sure Jesus isn't asleep in your boat! You can try to row your boat or operate your ministry in your own strength, but you'll not get far while Jesus is sleeping. The disciples found that "*the waves broke over the boat, so that it was nearly swamped*" (Mark 4:37, emphasis added). Wake Jesus up and make Him the Lord and Master of everything you do! Too many churches and ministries have welcomed Jesus into their midst in the past, but today they are operating in their own strength and making their own plans while Jesus sleeps in their midst.

God wants all Christians to be fishers of men. The world is in a desperate, destructive mess. Nations wage war on each other, and every day people inflict unmentionable cruelty on one another. If we have Jesus in our hearts, we are called to be fishermen, regardless of our background, education or economic position. Some individuals may be more gifted at fishing than we are, but Jesus is looking for those like Peter, James and John. They knew they were unworthy sinners, yet they were willing to trade their weakness for God's strength and their stained garments for robes of righteousness.

The apostles were largely uneducated, rough young men, yet God used them to shake the world with the gospel. If God was able to use them in such a way, we can never excuse ourselves from the personal responsibility we have to reach out to the lost. We can trick ourselves, and maybe even other people, but we can never deceive the Lord. Each Christian will one day give an account of the way they used, or didn't use, the talents God gave them.

Now is the time for us to commit ourselves fully to the cause of God, without reservation. If you do this, you will not fail to experience the blessing and presence of God in a sweet and powerful way.

When Jesus first found Peter, James and John, they were washing their fishing nets. From time to time it is necessary to clean our nets if we constantly use them to catch fish, but today many churches have become professional net washers. Instead of catching souls for the kingdom of God, they spend all their time talking about fishing, studying various fishing strategies and techniques, listening to the lectures of fishing experts, and singing songs about fishing. Yet they rarely, or never, actually go fishing!

Many pastors fill their pulpits with fishing stories, and their congregation admires the fishing nets that are displayed on the church walls. The nets have been thoroughly cleaned. No effort has been spared to keep all dirt and impurity out of the church. Indeed, the nets have been bleached so white that nobody would ever guess they had once been used for fishing! The strings are carefully arranged so that each square has the same size and shape. After all, they say, "God is a God of order." The pastors love to boast about their nets and even invite Christians from other churches to come and admire their nets with them.

Every few years "overzealous" young believers come in and suggest that they should take the nets down from the wall and take them out on the lake to catch some fish. The "mature" members of the congregation explain that God is catching many fish throughout the world, and all is well. Their job is to live holy, peaceful lives and not be presumptuous. The new believers are assured that once they have followed the Lord for a few more years, they will mature and become just like the others. For now, they had best remain quiet and stop speaking out of turn.

Week after week, year after year, Satan lulls individual believers, churches and whole denominations to sleep with his lies. The bleach that has removed all the stains and dirt from the nets also effectively disinfects the Christians until they never consider becoming fishermen again.

Christian, do you feel like Peter did after he worked all night but failed to catch a single fish? Have you convinced yourself that there are no more fish left in the sea? Have your church programs failed to net any new fish for so long that you would rather stay on the bank washing your nets, because one more failed fishing trip might be more than you can take? Many churches have given up on evangelism because they "tried it, and it didn't work."

Many Christians hear God's voice calling them to catch fish for the kingdom of God, but like Peter, James and John, they don't believe there are any fish left in the water. How often have you heard Christians say, "Nobody around here is interested in the gospel anymore," or "People's hearts are so hard"? This is not true! Have you ever considered that the problem might be that your fishing is not under the direction of the Lord Jesus Christ? Perhaps you have spent years casting your nets in the wrong place. I promise you that there are fish in the sea all around you. You need to stop fishing your way and start fishing under the direction of Jesus.

Peter caught nothing while he and his friends operated in

their own strength. They were convinced there were no fish left. But when they gave up and allowed God to direct their efforts, suddenly "they caught such a large number of fish that their nets began to break" (Luke 5:6).

Please understand this! When we try to serve the Lord and preach the gospel in our own strength, using our own programs and initiatives, we will fail and will soon convince ourselves the problem lies not with us, but with the "apathetic heathens" who "show no interest in the gospel." But when we learn what it truly means to give ourselves to God unreservedly, asking Him to fill and empower us, we will start to be in a place where God can use us for His glory. As long as you are looking for God to bless "your" ministry, you are wasting your time. He only blesses His ministry, done His way, by His leading. When we finally reach the end of all our useless programs and give up in desperation, Jesus will be there to show us a better way – His way. He will tell us where to throw our nets, and we will be amazed to see them bulging with fish.

Pastors, your church must get busy fishing, because this is what the church is meant to do. Jesus never intended His people to become insular and just sit around edifying each other. It is also not the job of a leader to spend all his time dealing with problems in the church. Of course there will always be problems until Jesus returns, but they should not bog you down. Instead, you should see them as opportunities to mend your net so that you can go fishing for souls with a stronger net.

The Devil will send all kinds of problems to distract you from fishing, so you need a firm and unwavering focus to win souls. Has your church given up trying to catch fish? Have you been busy cleaning your nets, convinced that there are no more fish left in the sea? The Word of God has some exciting news for you! Not only does God want to change you and empower your ministry, but after He does so, you will be a tremendous example for others to follow.

Are you also willing to let Jesus take control and make you a fisher of men? Let Jesus come into your boat and teach you. He can use your boat and net for His glory. God might have already given you a direction to preach the gospel. He might call you to Asia, Africa or some Muslim country as a witness to His beloved Son.

Now is the time to cast your net for fishing.

17

Sleeping Church, Awake!

> The hour has come for you to wake up from your slumber, because our salvation is nearer now than when we first believed.
>
> *Romans 13:11*

Before I left China in 1997, I had a very positive impression of Western Christianity. The missionaries who had come to China were very godly men and women. They put up with much opposition, and hundreds spilled their blood on Chinese soil for the sake of the gospel.

After I arrived in Germany, I was placed in a refugee facility while the government processed my application to stay. Every Sunday during those months, I walked to a Lutheran church in the neighborhood. I couldn't understand a word of German, and nobody in the church knew who I was, but I faithfully sat there each Sunday and observed the strange goings-on. The pastor climbed up into his elevated pulpit, while the congregation of four or five old women watched. He seemed to be carrying heavy burdens, and there was no joy or life in his face. He would read a prayer from a book and then preach for a while. I took the opportunity to try to mimic his words so that I might get used to this strange new language.

As soon as the service ended, the pastor rushed to the door so that he could shake the hands of the five or six of us who attended. I was very grieved by this whole strange process. It was clear that the pastor and his small flock all came to the meetings carrying the burdens of the world on their backs, and they all went home in exactly the same condition. I had grown up in the midst of revival in China, so it was a severe shock to me. Later I realized that not all churches in Germany or the West were quite as bad as this initial experience, but the true presence of Jesus is missing in most of them. Some churches might play louder music or appear energetic and joyful on the outside, but this does not necessarily mean they have the presence of Jesus in their hearts any more than the old Lutheran church. Jesus said, "The kingdom of God does not come with your careful observation, nor will people say, 'Here it is,' or 'There it is,' because the kingdom of God is within you" (Luke 17:20–21).

After being granted refugee status by the German authorities in 1998, the Lord started to open doors for me to minister around Europe and then in different parts of the world. From the start I understood that part of the reason God had allowed me to leave China was to help the sleeping Western church wake up! The message the Christians need to hear is the same that Jesus told the church in Sardis: "I know your deeds; you have a reputation of being alive, but you are dead. Wake up! Strengthen what remains and is about to die, for I have not found your deeds complete in the sight of my God. Remember, therefore, what you have received and heard; obey it, and repent" (Rev. 3:1–3).

A sleeping church can never reach a lost world.

The Bible declares all of humankind to be spiritually dead,

and they are drowning in an ocean of sin and wickedness. If they don't hear the gospel in their lifetime, then they are destined for everlasting punishment in hell. This is tragic, because Jesus said everlasting punishment in hell was "prepared for the devil and his angels" (Matt. 25:41), and not for people who were created in God's image and likeness.

The only way they will hear that Jesus has made a way for them to escape this dreadful destiny is if we tell them! Many Christians somehow think it is someone else's responsibility to tell the lost about Jesus. We make up numerous excuses to try to justify our inactivity and ease our consciences, but the Lord knows the truth. The Bible plainly instructs us to "rescue those being led away to death; hold back those staggering toward slaughter. If you say, 'But we knew nothing about this,' does not he who weighs the heart perceive it? Does not he who guards your life know it? Will he not repay each person according to what he has done?" (Prov. 24:11–12).

The time is short, and it will not do for Christians to continue to play games while millions of people around us are perishing and going to hell.

Believers often use Revelation 3:20 as an invitation to salvation. It says, "Here I am! I stand at the door and knock. If anyone hears my voice and opens the door, I will come in and eat with him, and he with me." Closer examination of this passage reveals that Jesus wasn't knocking at the door of unbelievers' hearts when he said those words. He was knocking at the door of the backslidden church at Laodicea. Jesus was standing outside the door of the church, knocking and asking to be let in! It's a sad indictment, but Jesus continues to be an unwelcome guest in many churches today. Many continue to operate in their lifeless religiosity, "having a form of godliness, but denying its power" (2 Tim. 3:5).

Wake up! Repent! Let the Lord Jesus come into your lives and into your churches. He loves all people, and as long as you have breath in you, it's not too late for Him to use you for His glory.

A spiritually dull church or believer is a poor witness for the living, resurrected Jesus. A church is meant to be a training centre and command hub for war, not a social club for pleasantries and hypocrisy, where people give lip service to Christ while refusing to obey His commands. Not only does God want you to wake up, but He has a work for you to do.

As I have traveled around the world, I have met many wonderful brothers and sisters. They listen intently to every word that is spoken, but there is one major thing missing in their spiritual lives. They need to start obeying the Word of God. They need to step out and start being doers of the Word instead of just listeners. James said, "Do not merely listen to the word, and so deceive yourselves. Do what it says" (James 1:22).

You see, when you only listen to the Word of God, your heart gets filled up with spiritual food. This is good, but it is there to serve a purpose. That purpose is for you to go and share the food you have with the hungry, so that they too can know Jesus. If you just keep God's blessings to yourself, you will become a bloated and sick Christian. When you share them with others, the Holy Spirit will give you more so that you can share more. It is a wonderful thing.

The greatest battle in the history of humankind is taking place right now. No, it's not the "war on terror," but a conflict far more intense and far-reaching! It is the battle for the souls of humankind. This war affects every single person in the world, for their eternal destinies depend on the result. Satan is busy trying to drag as many people to hell with him as possible. The Bible tells us, "Woe to the earth and the sea, because the devil has gone down to you! He is filled with fury, because he knows that his time is short" (Rev. 12:12).

If there has ever been a time on earth when the Devil's fury has been manifest so intensely, it is now. God's people should be busy doing their heavenly Father's work, serving Him and reaching out to the lost in whatever capacity God calls them to. Instead, millions of Christians are asleep, snoring away while they wait for the Lord to return!

If you have ever lived on a farm, you will know that the harvest needs workers to gather it in. Today the Lord wants to reap a harvest of souls for His kingdom, but there are not enough obedient workers. In this context the book of Proverbs gives the following warnings: "He who gathers crops in summer is a wise son, but he who sleeps during harvest is a disgraceful son" (Prov. 10:5); and "A sluggard does not plow in season; so at harvest time he looks but finds nothing" (Prov. 20:4).

It's time to wake up! "Wake up, O sleeper, rise from the dead, and Christ will shine on you" (Eph. 5:14).

There are more than 2,000,000,000 professing Christians in the world today. Think about that: two thousand million people who say they follow Jesus Christ! That is a staggering number.

So why then are there still so many needy countries and areas of spiritual darkness in the world today? The problem lies in the kind of Christianity practiced by the majority of believers today. For countless millions of people, following Jesus is little more than a cultural experience. Joining a church means little more than joining a social club where they can meet new people and exchange pleasantries about inconsequential matters. If the Bible is read at all, it is from a sense of duty rather than as part of a relationship with its real, vibrant and life-changing Author.

Jesus is often portrayed as a historical figure who died on the cross and as a future figure who will one day come again, but few Christians really, genuinely walk with Jesus today, sharing their dreams, fears and concerns with Him as a lover and friend. Millions of believers around the world are bound by legalism. Obeying man-made rules has become more important than taking the hand of God and walking with Him in the cool of the evening. The Christian life has become an endurance test, and all traces of life and joy have long since evaporated!

Brothers and sisters, don't be deceived; such a bound church will never be able to save any souls for the kingdom of God. They will only respond when they are confronted with the truth and grace of God's Word as revealed in the lives of true disciples of Jesus who have given up all they have to follow Him.

There are more than enough "believers" in the world today. God wants more disciples! Only disciples of Jesus can ever hope to impact the nations for God.

Several years ago the deadly SARS virus was spreading across China and parts of Asia. Scientists believe the epidemic was spread by "super-carriers." These super-carriers infected hundreds of people just by interacting with them. Everywhere they went they spread the virus, and people's lives were changed forever.

God is looking for super-carriers of the gospel! He wants wholehearted followers who are willing to take the fire and love of God to millions of people who will be infected with spiritual life!

Prior to the 1950s, most Christians in China were also mere "believers" in Christ, and when the heat of affliction came on, many fell away from the faith. Others, however, became serious about God and decided to follow Him regardless of the cost. They were gradually transformed into disciples of the Lord Jesus Christ. Today most Christians in China's house churches are disciples.

True disciples are often misunderstood. They are viewed as unstable fanatics. Often the same governments that tolerate the existence of mere believers will stop at no end to completely eradicate any disciples from within their borders.

"Believers" try to follow God, but their prayers and commitment are clouded with indecisiveness. Their prayers go like this: "Oh Lord, I am so weak. Please send Your power. I am weighed down with sin. Please come and relieve me." "Believers" always seek assurance that nothing will go wrong if they step out for Jesus. Only when they are convinced that the coast is clear and no harm will befall them are they willing to take their first step! If they ever hear the King's call to go somewhere and do something for the sake of His kingdom, they feel they need extra encouragement before they can safely step out: "First let me check with my wife, my pastor, my boss and my mother-in-law to see if it's all right with them."

"Disciples" have a different attitude. They beg God to give them just a little of His dynamite power. They pray, "Oh God, if you will lend me just a little spiritual dynamite, I promise I will take it to the darkest area I can find, place it there and pray You will send Your fire from heaven to explode it."

God always does. This is why the gospel is spreading so quickly in China and in other parts of the world.

Since coming to the West, I have found it doesn't really matter how much you preach in most churches, because the majority of believers have become "sermon proof". They have listened to thousands of sermons and have become experts at tuning out. Their bodies are physically in front of you, but their minds and hearts are far away. They have been conditioned to listen to speeches rather than to respond to the power of the gospel and be changed. Often there is a huge difference between the appearance believers put on every Sunday at church and the reality of their lives at home and work during the week. It is unhealthy to smile and act holy on Sunday when your family is falling apart, your marriage is breaking down and your life is swamped with sin and temptations. This is not real. The church should be the place where you encounter God and He changes you from darkness to light and from death to life. Fellowship with other believers should bring encouragement and inspiration as we become real with one another and seek to walk together in the kingdom of God. We need to bring the homes together with the churches so that how people act on Sunday becomes consistent with the reality of their daily lives.

Many churches in the West have been reduced to mere performances where the pastor puts on a show every week and the believers sit there as non-participating spectators. No wonder so many are struggling and falling away from the faith. The Lord is roused to anger when the precious bride of Christ falls into such a lamentable condition. Jesus is passionate for His bride. He "gave himself up for her to make her holy, cleansing her by the washing with water through the word, and to present her to himself as a radiant church, without stain or wrinkle or any other blemish, but holy and blameless" (Eph. 5:25–27).

If you are a pastor who shepherds the flock in this kind of way, I exhort you to come down from behind your pulpit and be with the people. Stop lecturing them and begin living with them, sharing in their burdens and guiding them to Jesus through the power of the Holy Spirit. Do not think you have some kind of privileged role in the church or that you are higher than anyone else, for we are all fellow pilgrims, and God does not show favoritism.

The role of a church leader is not to lord it over people and dominate gatherings, but rather it is to serve the brothers and sisters so that they, in turn, will be better prepared to serve the Lord and proclaim the gospel. You may have read these verses a thousand times, but I challenge you to read them again, prayerfully, and ask God to show you if your ministry truly reflects the apostle Paul's teaching: "It was he who gave some to be apostles, some to be prophets, some to be evangelists, and some to be pastors and teachers, to prepare God's people for works of service, so that the body of Christ may be built up until we all reach unity in the faith and in the knowledge of the Son of God and become mature, attaining to the whole measure of the fullness of Christ" (Eph. 4:11–13).

My precious friend, God loves you. He wants you to become a wholehearted disciple of Jesus, not merely a believer. Every Christian on earth has this choice to make every morning of their life. Whether we are a disciple or a believer depends on the choices we make. The temptation is for us to ease back into our comfortable chair and continue to live a halfhearted Christian life, giving lip service to God but being unwilling to count the cost and take up our cross and follow Him.

I pray that you will determine in your heart to follow Jesus with all your heart from this moment forward. You may face great hardship and come under constant attack, but you will never regret it.

18

A Worldwide Vision

Before I first traveled to the West in 1997, I had absolutely no idea that so many churches were spiritually asleep. I presumed the Western church was strong and vibrant because it had brought the gospel to my country with such incredible faith and tenacity. Many missionaries were a powerful example to us by laying down their lives for the sake of Jesus.

On occasions I've struggled while speaking in Western churches. There seems to be something missing that leaves me feeling terrible inside. Some meetings are cold and lack the fire and presence of God that we have in China.

In the West many Christians have an abundance of material possessions, yet they live in a backslidden state. They have silver and gold, but they don't rise up and walk in Jesus' name. In China we have few possessions to hold us down, so there's nothing preventing us from serving the Lord. The Chinese church is like Peter at the Beautiful Gate. When he saw the crippled beggar, he said, "Silver or gold I do not have, but what I have I give you. In the name of Jesus Christ of Nazareth, walk" (Acts 3:6).

In a similar way, I pray God might use the Chinese church to help the Western church rise up and walk in the power of the Holy Spirit. It's almost impossible for the Christians in China to go to sleep in the country's present environment. There's always something to keep us on the run, and it's very difficult to sleep while you're running. If persecution stops, I fear we will become complacent and fall asleep.

Many pastors in Europe and America have told me they want to see great revival. I'm frequently asked why China is experiencing revival while most countries in the West are not. This is a big question to answer, but some reasons are very apparent to me.

When I'm in the West, I see all the mighty church buildings and all the expensive equipment, plush carpets and state-of-the-art sound systems. I can assure the Western church with absolute certainty that you don't need any more church buildings. Church buildings will never bring the revival you seek. The pursuit of more possessions will also fail to bring revival. Jesus truly stated, "A man's life does not consist in the abundance of his possessions" (Luke 12:15).

The first thing needed for revival to return to your churches is the Word of the Lord. God's Word is missing. Sure, there are many preachers and thousands of tapes and videos of Bible teaching, but so little contains the sharp truth of the Bible, "for the word of God is living and active. Sharper than any double-edged sword, it penetrates even to dividing soul and spirit, joints and marrow; it judges the thoughts and attitudes of the heart" (Heb. 4:12). God's Word is the truth that will set you free.

Not only is knowledge of God's Word lacking, but obedience to that Word is lacking. Not much action is taking place.

From the time I first met the Lord Jesus Christ at the age of sixteen, I determined in my heart that I would be obedient to whatever He told me to do and say. This has not always been easy, but God has helped me each step of the way. When revival came to believers in China, the result was thousands of evangelists being sent out to all corners of the nation, carrying fire from the altar of God with them. When God moves in the West, it seems you want to stop and enjoy His presence and blessings too long and build an altar to your experiences.

You can never really know the Scriptures until you're willing to be changed by them. All true revivals of the Lord result in believers responding with fervent prayer and action for the lost. When God truly moves in your heart, you cannot remain silent.

I've seen people in Western churches worshiping like they're already in heaven. Then someone invariably brings a comforting message like, "My children, I love you. Don't be afraid; I'm with you." I'm not opposed to such words, but why is it that nobody seems to hear a word from the Lord like, "My child, I want to send you to the slums of Asia or the darkness of Africa to be my messenger to people dying in their sin"?

Multitudes of church members in the West are satisfied with giving their minimum to God instead of their maximum. I've watched men and women during offering time in church. They open their fat wallets and search around for the smallest amount they can give. This type of attitude will never do! Jesus gave His whole life for us, and we give as little of our lives, time and money as we can back to God. What a disgrace! Repent!

Giving to God's work is a great privilege. When the wise men traveled to Bethlehem, they brought costly gifts and placed them at the feet of the infant Jesus. Perhaps these gifts helped pay for Jesus and His parents to escape to Egypt a short time later.

God can use what you give Him to extend the reign of His Son throughout the world.

This may sound strange, but I even miss the offerings we used to give in China. On numerous occasions the leader would announce, "We have a new worker who is leaving tomorrow to serve the Lord." Immediately every single person would completely empty their pockets of everything they had. With that money the worker would buy a train or bus ticket and leave the next day.

In China today most of the house church believers do not own much. Most are from poor farming communities and struggle to survive from one harvest to the next. Whatever they do have, however, they give to God. There is no holding back. I remember some services when a small sack was passed around to collect the offering so that our evangelists could go to remote areas with the gospel. Many put everything they had in this world into the sack, for they realized nothing was more important than to participate in the saving of souls for Jesus. Even if it meant they would go without and face hardship, they were more than willing to do so if it meant just one more precious soul might be saved for all eternity.

On some occasions the sack would reach a man or woman who had nothing to put into it; they had no money or worldly possessions at all. All they had was themselves. I have witnessed men and women, with tears streaming from their eyes, literally get into the offering sack when it passed them, for they wanted to signal to God that their lives are all they have to give and they are willing to give them for His glory.

How about you?

Will you also give all of your heart to Jesus?

If you do, you will see God's glory and experience His

power and authority, for when God sees a heart that is fully devoted to Him, He is moved. The Bible declares, "For the eyes of the LORD range throughout the earth to strengthen those whose hearts are fully committed to him" (2 Chron. 16:9).

This sick world desperately needs to experience the love and grace of Jesus Christ. Those who already love Him must give their lives wholeheartedly to His cause, for nothing less will suffice.

Of course, not all Western churches are asleep! Of all the strong churches I have visited in the West, I've noticed one thing they all have in common: a strong and sacrificial commitment to missions among unreached nations. I'm not talking just about local outreach, or even attempts to start churches in other cities in your nation. I'm talking about a heart to establish God's kingdom in the most gospel-starved and spiritually dark areas of the world, where nobody has ever heard the name of Jesus. When you start putting your time, prayers and finances there, you will soon experience God's blessing on the work of your hands.

If your vision for the Lord has been too small, then ask Him to share *His* vision with you. You will find that the vision of God is a worldwide one, "for God so loved the world that he gave his one and only Son, that whoever believes in him shall not perish but have eternal life. For God did not send his Son into the world to condemn the world, but to save the world through him" (John 3:16–17).

The Great Commission has not changed. It is our plans that need to be changed. There are many churches trying to create a heaven here on earth, but until the Western church obeys the Great Commission and takes the gospel to the ends of the earth, people are just playing with God and are not really serious about the Truth. Many churches look beautiful on the outside but are dead where it counts, on the inside. If you truly want to see God move, the two main things you must do are learn the Word of God and have the obedience to do what God tells you to do.

As you step out in obedience to God, don't think you are all alone. God wants you to work alongside other members of His body, both for your own benefit and because by cooperating with others, you can achieve much more for God's kingdom than if you try to function alone.

When we get isolated we can open ourselves up to a loss of perspective that can cause us to make incorrect decisions. Elijah was a servant of God who knew both the highs and lows of ministry. One day he saw fire fall from the sky and burn up the offering he had soaked with twelve jars of water (1 Kings 18:16–39), and God brought a three-year drought to an end in answer to Elijah's prayers. A mighty victory was had for the kingdom of God, and the people of Israel were brought to repentance for their many years of idolatry and disobedience.

The very next day the wicked queen Jezebel threatened to murder Elijah before the sun went down. The man of God was full of fear and fled for his life into the desert, where he "came to a broom tree, sat down under it and prayed that he might die. 'I have had enough, Lord,' he said. 'Take my life; I am no better than my ancestors'" (1 Kings 19:4).

This should be a lesson to all servants of God. Often your most vulnerable point comes immediately after your greatest triumph. Not only must we give our failures to God, but we must give Him our successes also. Each day we need to start afresh, calling out to Him for help and strength.

Yesterday's victories will not sustain us in today's battle.

God had mercy on Elijah and provided food and strength for him. The prophet traveled all the way to Mount Horeb, which is also known as Sinai, the mountain where Moses received the Ten Commandments. When the Lord graciously spoke to the burnt-out Elijah, He asked, "What are you doing here, Elijah?" (1 Kings 19:13).

Elijah's response is very interesting. He said, "I have been very zealous for the LORD God Almighty. The Israelites have rejected your covenant, broken down your altars, and put your prophets to death with the sword. I am the only one left, and now they are trying to kill me too" (1 Kings 19:14).

Elijah believed he was the only prophet of God left alive.

Was that true?

A short time earlier Elijah had met Obadiah, who told him, "I hid a hundred of the LORD's prophets in two caves, fifty in each, and supplied them with food and water" (1 Kings 18:13). The very same day, however, Elijah told King Ahab, "I am the only one of the LORD's prophets left" (18:22). When Elijah reminded God that he was the last remaining prophet, the gentle voice of the Almighty replied, "I reserve seven thousand in Israel—all whose knees have not bowed down to Baal and all whose mouths have not kissed him" (19:18).

Often if we become isolated as we follow the Lord, we lose a correct sense of perspective and start to think we are the only ones in the battle and that the whole world is arrayed against us. It is interesting that after he lost perspective, Elijah was commanded to appoint Elisha to replace him. His ministry had come to an end.

As you go forth in obedience to the Great Commission, pray earnestly that God will show you whom you should go with. When it comes to serving the Lord, we should always connect with other members of the body of Christ, lest, like Elijah, we lose perspective and start to think we are the only true servant of God left in the land. Even if you are the most gifted Christian in the world, you cannot serve God in isolation. The disciples were always sent out in pairs, and the apostle Paul never traveled alone but always had coworkers with him.

We need to be encouraged by others who are walking with us on the journey. Discouragement is like a disease. It can strip you of all energy and peace and cause you to become cynical. *Dis-courage-ment* is just that. It breeds the opposite of courage, making us weak and fearful. In many places throughout the Bible, the Lord exhorts His people to "be strong and courageous." We all need encouragement from the messengers of God. He has many ways to lift up the heads of His downcast children. When Elijah was discouraged, God twice sent an angel with bread and water, which strengthened him for the long journey ahead (see 1 Kings 19:3–8). Today we need the living water of the Holy Spirit to overflow us, bringing refreshment and strength for our journey.

Your gifts need to be complemented with those of other members of God's family. The Bible teaches:

> *Now the body is not made up of one part but of many. If the foot should say, "Because I am not a hand, I do not belong to the body," it would not for that reason cease to be part of the body. And if the ear should say, "Because I am not an eye, I do not belong to the body," it would not for that reason cease to be part of the body....*
>
> *God has combined the members of the body and has given greater honor to the parts that lacked it, so that there should be no division in the body, but that its parts should have equal*

concern for each other. If one part suffers, every part suffers
with it; if one part is honored, every part rejoices with it.

1 Corinthians 12:14–16, 24–26

I encourage you to bow in prayer and ask the Holy Spirit to give you God's heart for the world. Pray that you may have a worldwide vision and love for the nations as Jesus does. Then ask that He might give you the sensitivity to hear His voice and the determination to obey His call.

I know that when you gain a worldwide vision for God's kingdom, your life will be full of purpose and will never lack direction again.

19

Chocolate Soldiers

A chocolate Christian dissolves in water and melts at the smell of fire. Living their lives in a glass dish or in a cardboard box, each clad in his soft clothing, a little frilled white paper to preserve his dear little constitution.... God never was a chocolate manufacturer and never will be. God's men are always heroes. In Scripture you can trace their giant foot-tracks down the sands of time.

C. T. Studd

All throughout the Scriptures we read about how God used people to accomplish His purposes on the earth. We read numerous accounts of how God transformed normal people into warriors for His kingdom. Brave and courageous men were always honored both by God and by the community. Often the Bible mentions such people in passing, such as, "All these were descendants of Asher—heads of families, choice men, brave warriors and outstanding leaders ... men ready for battle" (1 Chron. 7:40).

Strangely, in some churches today Jesus Christ is portrayed as a sensitive, weak and emotional man. While Jesus is symbolized as a lamb, we should not forget that He is also symbolized as a lion! The Jesus who gently played with little children and gathered them to His lap also made a whip and caused a riot in the temple courts.

Jesus is tough, manly, noble and the personification of courage. He is a warrior of the highest rank, the Commander in Chief of the Lord's armies, the one with fire in His eyes and a double-edged sword in His hand.

Millions of Christian women around the world are lamenting the absence of strong and godly Christian men in the church.

Jesus is too.

God wants more warriors in His church. He is looking for people who are serious about Him, who are strong in character and integrity and who are disciplined like soldiers. Did you know that "the eyes of the LORD range throughout the earth to strengthen those whose hearts are fully committed to him" (2 Chron. 16:9)? In China I have known many courageous men and women of God. They have been so overwhelmed by the love of God that they have no hesitation in dedicating the rest of their lives to do whatever it takes, and whatever it costs, to see as many people as possible know Jesus.

Caleb was one man who had a warrior spirit in him. He was not just a physical warrior, but all of his battles were also fought in the spiritual realm as he had to deal with numerous situations requiring the Lord's wisdom and guidance. The spirit of a warrior is not dimmed by age or time. Even near the end of his life, Caleb declared, "Now then, just as the LORD promised, he has kept me alive for forty-five years since the time he said this to Moses, while Israel moved about in the desert. So here I am today, eighty-five years old! I am still as strong today as the day Moses sent me out; I'm just as vigorous to go out to battle now as I was then" (Josh. 14:10–11).

Often preachers talk about how God wants to "raise up an army," but in many parts of the Bible we see that God was first and foremost interested in raising up an individual, and from that individual came great deliverance for God's people. We can see this in His dealings with Moses, Noah, David, Elijah, Jeremiah, Paul and so on.

Quantity is never as important to God as quality. He doesn't need an army of people to accomplish His purposes. Just a few obedient servants with the anointing of the Holy Spirit on their lives can bring about great things for the kingdom of God.

In the book of Judges we find a wonderful story of how God routed the Midianites with quality rather than with quantity. God had already told Gideon to strike down the Midianites (see Judg. 6:16). A large army mobilized to fight against the enemy forces, but God surprised Gideon by announcing, "You have too many men for me to deliver Midian into their hands. In order that Israel may not boast against me that her own strength has saved her, announce now to the people, 'Anyone who trembles with fear may turn back and leave Mount Gilead'" (Judg. 7:2–3).

Twenty-two thousand soldiers turned back that day.

Be careful not to miss the reason why God wanted to shrink this army to a smaller size. He was concerned that Israel might boast that their own strength had saved them once the victory was completed. Our God has declared, "I am the LORD; that is my name! I will not give my glory to another" (Isa. 42:8).

Gideon's original army of 32,000 men had decreased by more than two-thirds, but God was not finished. By observing whether the men knelt down and drank water from the spring of Harod with their hands or lapped it up like dogs, God refined the number of eligible soldiers down to a paltry 300!

To the natural mind this situation was hopeless. How could 300 men defeat the entire Midianite army that was boldly arrayed against it? To God, however, this represented no problem at all, for "nothing can hinder the LORD from saving, whether by many or by few" (1 Sam. 14:6).

Oh, if we could just catch a glimpse of His power and greatness, we would never be the same again! When the Lord is involved, He "will grant that the enemies who rise up against you will be defeated before you. They will come at you from one direction but flee from you in seven" (Deut. 28:7). Moses asked, "How could one man chase a thousand, or two put ten thousand to flight, unless their Rock had sold them, unless the LORD had given them up? For their rock is not like our Rock, as even our enemies concede" (Deut. 32:30–31).

There are certain men and women in the Bible who knew about God's greatness, and they were completely unafraid of what evil men could do to them. One of my favorite stories is that of Elisha and his servant Gehazi when the king of Aram decided to capture the prophet. The Bible records that "an army with horses and chariots had surrounded the city" (2 Kings 6:15).

Can you imagine that? How would you feel if an enraged king sent his whole army to kill you, and you were surrounded on every side?

Elisha had a deep revelation of God's greatness, and he walked by faith and not by sight. When his terrified servant asked what they should do, Elisha calmly replied, "Don't be afraid. Those who are with us are more than those who are with them" (2 Kings 6:16). He then prayed, "'O LORD, open his eyes so he may see.' Then the LORD opened the servant's eyes, and he looked and saw the hills full of horses and chariots of fire all around Elisha" (2 Kings 6:17). Elisha then prayed that the Lord would strike his enemies with blindness, and He did. The prophet and his servant continued on in their ministry. Because of this miracle, "the bands from Aram stopped raiding Israel's territory" (6:23).

Child of God, do you have a glimpse of how great Jesus is in your life? Do not be afraid of the Devil, for he is merely like a dog on a leash. God allows the Devil to attack us from time to time to keep us sharp, but he can never destroy us, for "the one who is in you is greater than the one who is in the world" (1 John 4:4). The Lord Jesus said of his followers, "I give them eternal life, and they shall never perish; no one can snatch them out of my hand. My Father, who has given them to me, is greater than all; no one can snatch them out of my Father's hand. I and the Father are one" (John 10:28–30).

God is calling for disciples who are steadfast warriors of the gospel. They may not look like warriors on the outside, but that is not what matters. What matters is what can be found on the inside, for "the LORD does not look at the things man looks at. Man looks at the outward appearance, but the LORD looks at the heart" (1 Sam. 16:7).

There are many Christians today who look like warriors for the Lord on the outside, but in reality they are chocolate soldiers, about whom the Bible says, "If you falter in times of trouble, how small is your strength!" (Prov. 24:10).

A chocolate soldier outwardly looks the same as a real soldier until the heat comes on him. All of a sudden he starts to feel uneasy; fear takes control, and he melts into a pile. A chocolate soldier looks strong while conditions are favorable, but when he is placed under pressure he collapses because he is empty inside. Jesus talked about a man who receives the seed of the Word of God with joy, "but since he has no root, he lasts only a short time. When trouble or persecution comes because of the word, he quickly falls away" (Matt. 13:21).

The reality is that we are all chocolate soldiers until Jesus comes and starts to build a solid foundation in our lives. One of the key components to developing godly character and re-solve in our lives is persecution. Paul wrote, "We also rejoice in our sufferings, because we know that suffering produces per-severance; perseverance, character; and character, hope" (Rom. 5:3–4); and "Be on your guard; stand firm in the faith; be men of courage; be strong" (1 Cor. 16:13).

David was a man who made many mistakes earlier in his life. He fully changed, however, and part of his prayer of re-pentance was, "Create in me a pure heart, O God, and renew a steadfast spirit within me" (Ps. 51:10). David knew that his heart was unclean, and his spirit shaky. God answered his prayer, and the Psalms later record, "Blessed is the man who fears the LORD, who finds great delight in his commands.... He will have no fear of bad news; his heart is steadfast, trusting in the LORD. His heart is secure, he will have no fear; in the end he will look in triumph on his foes" (112:1, 7–8).

The Lord Jesus taught His disciples the benefits of "stand-ing firm" in the face of opposition: "All men will hate you because of me, but he who stands firm to the end will be saved" (Matt. 10:22); and "By standing firm you will gain life" (Luke 21:19). We are exhorted to "consider him who endured such opposition from sinful men, so that you will not grow weary and lose heart" (Heb. 12:3).

If you want to be a warrior for Jesus Christ, you will first need to submit to God and allow Him to build character, perseverance, endurance, patience, hope and courage into your life. These attributes are given to those who desire to serve the Lord, "so that the man of God may be thoroughly equipped for every good work" (2 Tim. 3:17).

The Lord Jesus wants to develop a holy stubbornness inside of you—one that refuses to buckle to Satan or compromise with the world. He wants to train you up as a true soldier for the gospel, and not a chocolate soldier who melts with fear when placed under pressure. Stand up right now and call on the Lord Jesus to change you from being a chocolate soldier to one who will "endure hardship ... like a good soldier of Christ Jesus" (2 Tim. 2:3).

As you begin to serve God wholeheartedly as a soldier of Jesus Christ, you will need living water to flow and refresh you and your colleagues in battle. The Bible contains a powerful story of how God sent water to save the combined armies of Judah and Israel as they went to fight against the Moabites. To reach the battle, the armies marched through the Desert of Edom. The harsh conditions took a toll, and "after a roundabout march of seven days, the army had no more water for themselves or for the animals with them" (2 Kings 3:9).

The parched Israelites stopped in a valley and sent messengers to ask Elisha what they should do. Elisha replied, "This is what the LORD says: You will see neither wind nor rain, yet this valley will be filled with water, and you, your cattle and your other animals will drink. This is an easy thing in the eyes of the LORD; he will also hand Moab over to you" (2 Kings 3:17–18).

Even if you find yourself in a spiritual desert and hear death knocking at your door, God is able to send a flow of His living water to you. There is nowhere on earth that God cannot reach you. Even though the armies were stuck in the middle of a barren desert, "the next morning, about the time for offering the sacrifice, there it was—water flowing from the direction of Edom! And the land was filled with water" (2 Kings 3:20).

This was not a small trickle of water that God sent to help His warriors. It seems it was more like a large lake, because the next morning the Moabites saw the reflection of the rising sun in the water from a distance, and thought it was a huge pool of blood. They raced down to collect the plunder only to be routed by the Israelites. As you enter the battle against Satan and his forces, God's living water will give you the edge you need to rout the enemy. Stand firm, and don't become like a chocolate soldier. There will be times during the battle when you will desperately need God's intervention. You should stop and seek the Lord, and He will provide living water to refresh and invigorate you.

Let's conclude by prayerfully reading what is probably the greatest Bible passage referring to how the servant of God should be equipped for battle. As you read it, ask the Lord Jesus to equip and arm you so that you become a mighty warrior for His kingdom.

> *Finally, be strong in the Lord and in his mighty power. Put on the full armor of God so that you can take your stand against the devil's schemes. For our struggle is not against flesh and blood, but against the rulers, against the authorities, against the powers of this dark world and against the spiritual forces of evil in the heavenly realms. Therefore put on the full armor of God, so that when the day of evil comes, you may be able to stand your ground, and after you have done*

everything, to stand. Stand firm then, with the belt of truth buckled around your waist, with the breastplate of righteousness in place, and with your feet fitted with the readiness that comes from the gospel of peace. In addition to all this, take up the shield of faith, with which you can extinguish all the flaming arrows of the evil one. Take the helmet of salvation and the sword of the Spirit, which is the word of God. And pray in the Spirit on all occasions with all kinds of prayers and requests. With this in mind, be alert and always keep on praying for all the saints.

Ephesians 6:10–18

Part 3

Soldiers for Christ

&mbracing Juffering

> Do not be ashamed to testify about our Lord, or
> ashamed of me his prisoner. But join with me in suffering
> for the gospel, by the power of God.
>
> *2 Timothy 1:8*

*T*wo thousand years ago the Lord Jesus stood on the Mount of Olives and commanded His disciples to "go into all the world and preach the good news to all creation. Whoever believes and is baptized will be saved, but whoever does not believe will be condemned" (Mark 16:15–16).

On that wonderful Ascension Day, the Lord set in motion a process whereby His church would expand from its genesis in Jerusalem until it encompassed the globe, even to the ends of the earth.

I have some good news. You may have heard that the glorious gospel traveled around the world and reached my country, China. The power of the Holy Spirit touched our nation in a mighty way, and multitudes of people have come to love and trust the Lord Jesus! This has all been the doing of our heavenly Father, and all glory goes to Him alone.

For two generations the believers in China have been like

caged birds, as the government has tried to control us and limit the spread of the gospel. By the grace of God, however, I can tell you there are tens of millions of birds in China today who refuse to be caged! They have been set free by Jesus, and they refuse to live another day inside a man-made cage. They have started flying about to other countries, carrying the gospel with them wherever they go!

The Back to Jerusalem vision is not specifically about Jerusalem, as some people have thought. The main thrust of our vision is rather the lost millions of Muslims, Buddhists and Hindus who live in the many countries between China and Jerusalem. We believe each of the thousands of people groups living in these lands is precious to God, and He wants them to hear about the sacrifice and resurrection of His beloved Son. Indeed, we believe by proclaiming the gospel to the most resistant and least evangelized, we will be helping to complete the Great Commission, for Jesus said, "And this gospel of the kingdom will be preached in the whole world as a testimony to all nations, and then the end will come" (Matt. 24:14).

Regarding Israel, the Bible also says, "Israel has experienced a hardening in part until the full number of the Gentiles has come in. And so all Israel will be saved, as it is written: 'The deliverer will come from Zion; he will turn godlessness away from Jacob'" (Rom. 11:25–26).

The church in China believes that God has given us a role to play in the end times: to take the power and grace of the gospel to the House of Muhammad, the House of Buddha and the House of Hindu. Hundreds of millions of lost people are perishing there with little or no light of the gospel, and this is something that must change! God loves all people equally, and His glory must be revealed to all nations before the end will come. We want to see the "full number of Gentiles" come into God's kingdom! This is our call and passion, and we won't stop until what Habakkuk prophesied comes to pass: "For the earth will be filled with the knowledge of the glory of the LORD, as the waters cover the sea" (Hab. 2:14).

At the moment the whole earth is not filled with the knowledge of the glory of God. There are millions of people dying who have never even heard once in their lives that Jesus Christ came, bled for them on a cross and died and was buried for their sins. They have never heard that on the third day God's mighty power raised Jesus from the dead. For countless generations God has looked down from heaven and waited for His children to obey the Great Commission, to bring liberty to all held captive by the Devil. It is time for God's people everywhere to do whatever they can to complete the Great Commission and hasten the return of the King of Glory.

In China we realize that it is not going to be easy to take the gospel to these countries. Satan has bound the inhabitants of the Middle East, Central Asia, India and other places for thousands of years, and he will not let his captives go without a tremendous fight. We praise God, however, for He has equipped us with all the power and authority necessary to overthrow Satan's kingdom! Jesus asked, "How can anyone enter a strong man's house and carry off his possessions unless he first ties up the strong man? Then he can rob his house" (Matt. 12:29).

Through prayer and the proclamation of the gospel, we can tie up the strong man, Satan. But there is another weapon we can use to overpower the Devil—the weapon of suffering.

Just a few decades ago there were very few Christians in China, and many missionaries found it difficult to reach anyone with the gospel. But the heavenly Father had other ideas, for He wanted His Son to receive the glory of a redeemed bride in China. What started as a spark grew to a small flame, and the Holy Spirit fed the flames with generous doses of flammable oil until the revival became a mighty, all-consuming fire!

Around 100,000,000 people have given their lives to Jesus and have been overwhelmed by His love and goodness. They in turn could not help but take this good news to as many people as possible. The fire of God was, and still is, like a heavenly virus to many Christians in China. If they don't share it with others, they feel they will go crazy! It's just like Jeremiah, who said, "If I say, 'I will not mention him or speak any more in his name,' his word is in my heart like a fire, a fire shut up in my bones. I am weary of holding it in; indeed, I cannot" (Jer. 20:9).

Have you ever experienced God like this? Has the Holy Spirit ever burdened you in such a way that it was painful for you until you had a chance to share His Word with someone?

I think many Christians will say they want to experience God in this kind of way, but do you know what the verses say that immediately precede this proclamation by Jeremiah? Let's see what kind of life he was having that caused him to be so zealous for God that it pained him to hold his message in: "O LORD, you deceived me, and I was deceived; you overpowered me and prevailed. I am ridiculed all day long; everyone mocks me. Whenever I speak, I cry out proclaiming violence and destruction. So the word of the LORD has brought me insult and reproach all day long" (Jer. 20:7–8).

Jeremiah was being ridiculed, mocked, insulted and reproached "all day long," yet he testified that God's Word was like a fire in his heart and a fire shut up in his bones.

In China we always teach five things that all disciples need to be ready to do at any time. We need to be ready to pray, regardless of the circumstances. We must always be ready to share the gospel and always ready to suffer for the name of Jesus. We also teach every disciple in China that they must be ready to die for Jesus Christ, and finally they should be ready to escape for the gospel if the opportunity presents itself, for Jesus said, "When you are persecuted in one place, flee to another" (Matt. 10:23).

There is a great power when we suffer for the gospel. Countless believers in China have been brutally tortured, imprisoned and even killed for the gospel, but the church has continued to advance. The early believers in the book of Acts were similarly empowered and emboldened through their experiences of suffering. After a number of the apostles were thrown into jail, God provided a supernatural deliverance. The members of the Sanhedrin were baffled and wondered how they had escaped. The next morning they thought the apostles would have scattered into hiding, but "then someone came and said, 'Look! The men you put in jail are standing in the temple courts teaching the people.' At that, the captain went with his officers and ... made them appear before the Sanhedrin to be questioned by the high priest. 'We gave you strict orders not to teach in this name,' he said. 'Yet you have filled Jerusalem with your teaching and are determined to make us guilty of this man's blood.' Peter and the other apostles replied: 'We must obey God rather than men!'" (Acts 5:25–29).

Suffering produced boldness, which caused the kingdom of God to advance and the Devil's plans to be thwarted.

On the same day that Stephen was stoned to death, the Bible records that "a great persecution broke out against the church at Jerusalem, and all except the apostles were scattered throughout Judea and Samaria" (Acts 8:1). What was the result of this persecution and scattering of the believers? "Those who had been scattered preached the word wherever they went" (Acts 8:4). Great signs and wonders occurred wherever the Christians proclaimed the gospel, and so many people were added to the church that sometime later the Jews said of Paul and Silas, "These who have turned the world upside down have come here too" (Acts 17:6 NKJV).

In my own life I have also found that times of intense suffering for the gospel have led to a greater harvest of souls and more severe damage to the strongholds of Satan.

There are many ways the Lord may lead a Christian during his or her life, but I'm convinced that the path of every believer will sooner or later include suffering. The Lord gives us these trials to keep us humble and dependent on Him for our daily sustenance.

Don't be afraid of suffering, for it is how God's kingdom advances on the earth! The Bible instructs us in 1 Peter 4:1 that "since Christ suffered in his body, arm yourselves also with the same attitude, because he who has suffered in his body is done with sin."

How we mature as a Christian largely depends on the attitude we have when we're faced with suffering. Some try to avoid it or imagine it doesn't exist, but that only makes the situation worse. Others try to endure it grimly, hoping for relief. This is better but falls short of the full victory God wants to give each of His children.

The Lord wants us to embrace suffering as a friend. We need a deep realization that when we're persecuted for Jesus' sake, it is an act of God's blessing to us. This is why Jesus said,

"Blessed are you when people insult you, persecute you and falsely say all kinds of evil against you because of me. Rejoice and be glad, because great is your reward in heaven" (Matt. 5:11–12).

I have found over the years that many of the most fruitful times of ministry for the Lord have come at the same time as great opposition and persecution. There seems to be a direct correlation between effective work for God and intense opposition. The apostle Paul experienced this too. He wrote, "A great door for effective work has opened to me, and there are many who oppose me" (1 Cor. 16:9).

We can grow to such a place in Christ where we laugh and rejoice when people slander us, because we know we are not of this world, and our security is in heaven. The more we are persecuted for His sake, the more reward we will receive in heaven.

When people malign you, rejoice and be glad. When they curse you, bless them in return. When you walk through a painful experience, embrace it and you will be free! When you learn these lessons, there is nothing left that the world can do to you.

God is my witness that through all the tortures and beatings I've received, I have never hated my persecutors. Rather, I saw them as God's instruments of blessing and the vessels He chose to purify me and make me more like Jesus.

When a child of God suffers, you need to understand it is only because the Lord has allowed it. He has not forgotten you!

When I hear a house church Christian has been imprisoned for Christ in China, I don't advise people to pray for his or her release unless the Lord clearly reveals we should pray this way. Before a chicken is hatched, it is vital that it is kept in the warm protection of the shell for twenty-one days. If you take the chick out of that environment one day too early, it will die. Similarly, ducks need to remain confined in their shell for twenty-eight days before they are hatched. If you take a duck out on the twenty-seventh day, it will die.

There is always a purpose to why God allows His children to go to prison. Perhaps it's so they can witness to the other prisoners, or perhaps God wants to develop more character in their lives. But if we use our own efforts to get people out of prison earlier than God intended, we can thwart His plans, and the believer may come out not as fully formed as God wanted them to be.

The Lord told the apostle Paul, "My grace is sufficient for you, for my power is made perfect in weakness" (2 Cor. 12:9). This led Paul to declare, "Therefore I will boast all the more gladly about my weaknesses, so that Christ's power may rest on me. That is why, for Christ's sake, I delight in weaknesses, in insults, in hardships, in persecutions, in difficulties. For when I am weak, then I am strong" (12:9–10).

The kingdom of God advances through suffering.

21

Strength in the Storm

*I*f you want to be a soldier of Christ, you must be strong and bold. Being fearful and timid will never qualify you to be a soldier. A soldier of Christ can survive and carry out their God-given mission under any circumstances. A soldier of Christ also needs discipline, especially in the areas of prayer, Scripture reading and submission to His will. For whenever God gives a vision to His people, the Devil opposes it and does whatever he can to disrupt it. Satan does not care when Christians pursue their own visions and plans, but when God's Spirit is in operation, putting the pieces together for a strategic conquest of lost souls, Satan becomes alarmed and all kind of trouble breaks out.

As a young man, I started to preach the gospel, and I soon found a wave of trouble coming in my direction. Posters with my name and those of my coworkers were plastered all over the region, offering rewards for information leading to our capture. Thankfully China is a big place, so we just moved to a new location and continued to preach the gospel where the local authorities didn't know us.

The last several years have seen an enormous amount of opposition come to the Back to Jerusalem missionary effort.

Instead of being dismayed, we are fully persuaded that it is a vision from the heart of God, and what He begins He always completes! Paul encouraged the Philippians with the following words, which should also serve as an encouragement for us: "In all my prayers for all of you, I always pray with joy because of your partnership in the gospel from the first day until now, being confident of this, that he who began a good work in you will carry it on to completion until the day of Christ Jesus" (Phil. 1:4–6).

There are always doubters who come along to mock a move of God. Like Sanballat and Tobiah (Neh. 2:10–20), there are those who ridicule what they feel threatened by. There are others—like the ten spies—who could see nothing good in the Promised Land and looked on in bewilderment as Caleb reported to Moses, " 'We should go up and take possession of the land, for we can certainly do it.' But the men who had gone up with him said, 'We can't attack those people; they are stronger than we are.' And they spread among the Israelites a bad report about the land they had explored" (Num. 13:30–32). God himself later gave this testimony of Caleb: "Because my servant Caleb has a different spirit and follows me wholeheartedly, I will bring him into the land he went to, and his descendants will inherit it" (14:24).

I want to be like Caleb! I want to have a different spirit from the naysayers and critics who don't believe any good will happen unless they are directly involved. When it comes to serving God, we must never focus our attention on the size of the task, for it will squash our vision and enthusiasm. We should always place our eyes on the size of our Lord. What He says will happen always takes place in His perfect timing, and nothing can stop the Lord's will from being done on earth or in heaven! Our mighty God has declared, "My word that goes out from my mouth ... will not return to me empty, but will accomplish what I desire and achieve the purpose for which I sent it" (Isa. 55:11).

There are many good developments taking place with the Back to Jerusalem vision. Training is being conducted, and more Chinese believers are embracing the vision to preach the gospel to the giants of Islam, Buddhism and Hinduism. Yet at the same time I believe there is a kind of cancer among some of God's people today. It is a spiritual cancer of unbelief among many Christians. They can only see the giants and the difficulties and have become paralyzed with fear.

We must press on! We must press on because Back to Jerusalem is God's vision, not ours. If it originated with man, we would be condemned to failure, but it originated with God and we are assured of victory!

If you have a vision from God, then you don't need to be afraid! Be strong and courageous whenever people oppose you and the work God has called you to do. If you are not totally convinced that what you are doing has been born out of the will and plan of God, then your conviction will soon crumble and you will not move forward.

I am always encouraged by David's example of perseverance and faithfulness. His focus was firmly fixed on obeying God's will, and he didn't care about what others were doing or saying about him. The Bible records a remarkable account of when David and his men came home to Ziklag to discover the Amalekites had set fire to the town and carried off all of the women. What was the response of these mighty warriors? Did they immediately pray together and set out to recover their wives and daughters? No! The Bible says, "David and his men wept aloud until they had no strength left to weep" (1 Sam. 30:4).

When Satan uses people to attack and slander us, let's not sit around feeling sorry for ourselves and weeping until we feel like giving up. That will never accomplish God's purposes in our generation. Let's move forward in a spirit of forgiveness and meekness, but also of fire and determination. God's honor is at stake among the nations, and we must not be distracted from obeying our King.

After David's men had finished weeping, they started to think about their predicament and blamed David. This was the same David who had led them to victory after victory over the enemy. Yet when disillusionment set in, they quickly blamed their leader, even to the point of wanting to kill him! David "was greatly distressed because the men were talking of stoning him; each one was bitter in spirit because of his sons and daughters" (1 Sam. 30:6). I know how David felt. There have been times when my family and I have felt as if many among the church and mission establishment have hoisted large stones above their heads and would love nothing better than to crush us to death with their words and gossip.

Herein lies the secret to following God and pushing through the obstacles that Satan throws in your way: David didn't sit around arguing and discussing the problem with his men, nor did he try to convince them to change their minds. Instead, the Bible records, "David found strength in the LORD his God" (1 Sam. 30:6).

The enemy had stolen all the wives, children and possessions from David and his men. David asked God if they could recover them, and the Lord said, "Pursue them. You will certainly overtake them and succeed in the rescue" (1 Sam. 30:8). When God gives such a word, no demon in hell is able to stop it from coming to pass. It doesn't mean it will be easy, however, for even in the chase, 200 of David's men "were too exhausted to cross the ravine" (30:10).

God is able to do the impossible, and He will complete the Great Commission before Jesus returns to claim His inheritance. The prophet Ezekiel received a powerful vision in which he was shown a river flowing out of the temple of God. To start with, the water was ankle-deep. Then the angel measured off a thousand cubits, and the water was knee-deep. The level rose until it was up to Ezekiel's waist. In the fourth and final part of the vision, the angel "measured off another thousand, but now it was a river that I could not cross, because the water had risen and was deep enough to swim in—a river that no one could cross" (Ezek. 47:5).

In the first three levels, Ezekiel was able to stand up and walk in the water, but in the fourth level walking was completely impossible. The water was above his head, and the only way he could progress was by being carried along by God's current.

The gospel has gone throughout the world in a similar way. Jesus told His disciples, "You will receive power when the Holy Spirit comes on you; and you will be my witnesses in Jerusalem, and in all Judea and Samaria, and to the ends of the earth" (Acts 1:8). The gospel quickly advanced throughout Jerusalem, then into the surrounding areas of Judea. It soon saturated the region of Samaria. The final expansion of the kingdom of God—to the ends of the earth—cannot be achieved unless the river of the Holy Spirit picks us up and sweeps us along. The disciples were able to walk to Jerusalem, Judea and

Samaria, but there was no way they could walk to the ends of the earth. This could only be achieved if God helped them to do the impossible. This is the same today with the Back to Jerusalem vision. In our own strength we cannot penetrate the Muslim world with the gospel any more than a person can speak to a mountain and tell it to be cast into the sea. With God's help it will be done.

Many Christians have told me, "Brother Yun, we don't believe that God will give us impossible things to do. We believe He gives us things that we are able to do, and then we do it." This is nonsense! If you jump up and down and say, "I can do it! I can do it!" then it is not from the Lord at all. God gives us things that are absolutely impossible to do unless He is involved. That way He gets the glory when it is accomplished, and not us! When people hear about it, they don't say, "Look what those Christians did." Rather, they say, "Look at what God did!"

Consider all of the people whom God used to do mighty things throughout history. Was it possible for Moses to part the Red Sea with his staff? Or was it something only God could do, because He can do the impossible?

Was it possible for a young boy to slay Goliath?

Was it possible for Abraham and Sarah to have children at their advanced age, or Elijah to make fire fall from heaven and devour his waterlogged sacrifice in front of the prophets of Baal?

Was it because of their exertions that the Israelites saw the walls of Jericho fall to the ground when they marched around it, that Daniel shut the lions' mouths all night in the den, or that his friends survived being thrown into the fiery furnace?

We could go on with stories of Jonah and the disciples of

Jesus and the stirring accounts of the early church in the book of Acts.

God doesn't want you to merely do what you can. He wants you to believe Him to do what you cannot! Through such steps of faith the kingdom of God advances throughout the world.

One brother in China asked me how I "managed" to fast for seventy-four days during my first imprisonment in 1984. Many people have asked me the same question over the years, pointing out the obvious—that it is impossible for a person to last more than several days without food or water. I told the brother, "Surely you realize that fasting for such a length of time is totally impossible. Yet God's Spirit enabled me to survive, because "with man this is impossible, but not with God; all things are possible with God" (Mark 10:27).

Regarding my seventy-four-day fast in prison, I want to share with you that I didn't stop eating and drinking only as a spiritual exercise to get closer to the Lord. I had a second reason for undertaking the fast. The torture I had received in the prison was so severe that I decided it was better to die for the Lord than to continue. I felt frustrated because God had commanded me to preach the gospel to the West and South, but instead I found myself being brutally treated in a prison full of hopelessness and despair. In that dark time I decided it was better to die for the Lord if I could not fulfill His call on my life.

I told Jesus I was ready to come to Him, and I committed my spirit into His hands. Days went by, and then weeks. My body began to shrink from malnourishment, and I didn't say a word to anyone. I just lay there waiting for death so that I could enter into God's presence. For much of the time I experienced a wonderful intimacy with my heavenly Father. I meditated on Scriptures like, "I want to know Christ and the power of his resurrection and the fellowship of sharing in his sufferings, becoming like him in his death, and so, somehow, to attain to the resurrection from the dead" (Phil. 3:10–11).

The Lord, however, would not accept my sacrifice, and He sustained me by His supernatural power. His plan for me in this world had not been completed, and He allowed me to live. After seventy-four days my body had been so mistreated that I was little more than bones and skin. When my wife and family members came to the prison, they couldn't recognize me at first.

I have learned that God truly has power over life and death. It is our risen Lord Jesus who triumphantly declared, "I am the Living One; I was dead, and behold I am alive for ever and ever! And I hold the keys of death and Hades" (Rev. 1:18). I have come to realize that "in his hand is the life of every creature and the breath of all mankind" (Job 12:10). God is in complete control of the lives of His children, and indeed of all creation. Jesus assured us, "Are not two sparrows sold for a penny? Yet not one of them will fall to the ground apart from the will of your Father. And even the very hairs of your head are all numbered" (Matt. 10:29–30).

Many people foolishly think they are in control of their lives, and they waste a lot of time doing things they think will prolong their days on the earth. Yet King Solomon stated, "No man has power over the wind to contain it; so no one has power over the day of his death" (Eccl. 8:8). Dear brothers and sisters, please understand that the loving Creator has your life in the palm of His hand! When the Israelites thought God had forgotten them, He gave them this beautiful promise:

"Can a mother forget the baby at her breast
and have no compassion on the child she has borne?
Though she may forget,
I will not forget you!
See, I have engraved you on the palms of my hands;
your walls are ever before me."

Isaiah 49:15–16

Over the years God has been gracious to me, and I have come to understand that there is no life except in Jesus, no truth except in Jesus, and no way to do anything except through Jesus. We need a revelation of how great our Lord Jesus is! The Bible says, "He is the image of the invisible God, the firstborn over all creation. For by him all things were created: things in heaven and on earth, visible and invisible, whether thrones or powers or rulers or authorities; all things were created by him and for him. He is before all things, and in him all things hold together. And he is the head of the body, the church; he is the beginning and the firstborn from among the dead, so that in everything he might have the supremacy" (Col. 1:15–18).

As you hear the Word of God today, I pray you will be encouraged to stand up and follow Jesus Christ wholeheartedly. Don't give up, and never bow to opposition. It is merely there to test and refine us so we will be a more effective weapon in the hand of God. The apostle Paul frequently had the dual influences of opposition and effectiveness operating in his ministry. To the church in Corinth he wrote, "A great door for effective work has opened to me, and there are many who oppose me" (1 Cor. 16:9). Without opposition we will not be as effective as God wants us to be. Without persecution there would not have been revival in China, and without a crucifixion there would not have been a resurrection.

You can be certain that all Christians who dedicate their lives to preaching the gospel among the nations will be battered with many storms. Satan is not worried about most of the things promoted as Christian activity today, but he is always on the prowl when a follower of Jesus steps out in obedience to the Great Commission. After I made a commitment to obey God, all kinds of storms broke out, and over the years I have been arrested more than thirty times and have served the Lord in four different prisons. There are many brothers and sisters in China and other nations who have experienced even more storms than me.

The great news is that whenever you find yourself in the midst of a powerful storm, Jesus will appear and bring deliverance. On one occasion as the disciples feared for their lives in the midst of a raging storm, Jesus was so unworried that He was fast asleep in the back of the boat! "He got up and rebuked the wind and the raging waters; the storm subsided, and all was calm. 'Where is your faith?' he asked his disciples" (Luke 8:24–25).

Jesus is always the way forward. He is always the light at the end of our tunnel and the tower of strength to withstand the worst storms that the Devil can throw at us. It is *in Him* that we find strength, peace and overwhelming joy! I have learned that it doesn't matter what is going on around us or what fiery darts are aimed at us. They can never touch the life of Jesus that dwells in us. That is why so many thousands of martyrs throughout history have died courageous deaths in spite of cruel torture. There was a secret, hidden inner place that no man could touch and no flames could burn.

Let's pray for a new determination and a fresh vision. Ask the Lord to grant us strength to sustain us in the midst of fierce storms. Let us boldly "fix our eyes on Jesus, the author and perfecter of our faith, who for the joy set before him endured the cross, scorning its shame, and sat down at the right hand of the throne of God. Consider him who endured such opposition from sinful men, so that you will not grow weary and lose heart" (Heb. 12:2–3).

22

The God of Covenants

The Old Testament contains a wonderful story about King Jehoshaphat. This king was one of the few who was faithful to the Lord. I'm sure Jehoshaphat had many plans and projects on his mind, and when he lay in bed at night, his thoughts were probably already churning over those things his government would need to do the next day.

One morning, however, the king's plans were interrupted when a group of men arrived at the palace with alarming news: "A vast army is coming against you from Edom, from the other side of the Sea" (2 Chron. 20:2). All the king's plans went on hold, and he became frightened of this huge army that had come to destroy his kingdom.

Have you ever felt like Jehoshaphat did at that time? Have you been surrounded by enemies on every side, who wished to destroy you and demolish your ministry?

The first thing Jehoshaphat did after receiving this news was the key to his deliverance. The Scriptures record: "Alarmed, Jehoshaphat resolved to inquire of the LORD, and he proclaimed a fast for all Judah. The people of Judah came together to seek help from the LORD; indeed, they came from every town in Judah to seek him" (vv. 3–4). It would have been easy for Jehoshaphat to respond to the grave threat by urgently mobilizing his army and sending them out to meet the enemy head-on, but he wisely realized that he should not advance a single step until he sought the Lord and asked for His help. The king proclaimed a fast, and the men of Judah humbled themselves to seek the Lord.

It is a marvelous thing when God's people fast and pray together in unity. It moves the heart of the Lord. Food is the most basic of human needs. Satan knew this when he tempted Adam and Eve with food. To willfully deny yourself food in order to seek the Lord brings a great blessing to your life and circumstances.

Whenever you feel overwhelmed by the size and strength of the enemy's forces arrayed against you, withdraw and earnestly seek the face of Jesus just as Jehoshaphat and the people of Judah did. To earnestly seek God is a powerful act of faith. The Bible says, "Without faith it is impossible to please God, because anyone who comes to him must believe that he exists and that he rewards those who earnestly seek him" (Heb. 11:6).

It is important to note that the key thing here is that we seek *the Lord*. It's easy to seek resources, blessings or success. We must be careful, however, not to put these things first in our seeking. It is the Lord Jesus Christ we are to earnestly seek above all else. He taught, "But seek first his kingdom and his righteousness, and all these things will be given to you as well" (Matt. 6:33). The very next verse tells us, "Therefore do not worry about tomorrow, for tomorrow will worry about itself. Each day has enough trouble of its own" (v. 34).

King Jehoshaphat knew all about trouble. He was surrounded by a vast army that sought the destruction of his kingdom, yet he knew that his first priority was to seek the Lord and not to worry about tomorrow. The people of Judah realized that only God could rescue them from their dire predicament. They threw themselves on God's mercy and reminded the Almighty of the covenants He had made with their forefathers. Jehoshaphat stood up in the temple courtyard and cried out, "O LORD, God of our fathers, are you not the God who is in heaven? You rule over all the kingdoms of the nations. Power and might are in your hand, and no one can withstand you. O our God, did you not drive out the inhabitants of this land before your people Israel and give it forever to the descendants of Abraham your friend? They have lived in it and have built in it a sanctuary for your Name, saying, 'If calamity comes upon us, whether the sword of judgment, or plague or famine, we will stand in your presence before this temple that bears your Name and will cry out to you in our distress, and you will hear us and save us'" (2 Chron. 20:6–9).

God can never break His covenants. It is impossible for Him to do so. All the way through the Bible we read of God making covenants with people. He made a covenant with Noah and his family, and they were saved. He then made a covenant that He would never again destroy the earth by water and placed a rainbow in the sky as a reminder of His promise. He made covenants with Abraham, Isaac and Jacob for all generations. The fact that Israel has survived until the present day—despite being surrounded by nations that desire its destruction—serves as a powerful reminder of God's faithfulness to His covenants.

Moses knew that it was best to appeal to the character of God during times of trouble. He knew he could not appeal to God on the basis of the people's righteousness, for they would be destroyed. Instead, on several occasions he reminded God of His covenants. When God threatened to destroy the children of Israel after they fashioned an idol in the form of a golden calf, Moses cried out, "Remember your servants Abraham, Isaac and Israel, to whom you swore by your own self: 'I will make your descendants as numerous as the stars in the sky and I will give your descendants all this land I promised them, and it will be their inheritance forever.' Then the LORD relented and did not bring on his people the disaster he had threatened" (Ex. 32:13–14).

The apostle Paul taught that God's covenant with Israel was still in force. He reminded the Romans, "As far as the gospel is concerned, they are enemies on your account; but as far as election is concerned, they are loved on account of the patriarchs, for God's gifts and his call are irrevocable" (Rom. 11:28–29). Therefore, in God, Christians should love the people of Israel with whom God made an irrevocable covenant.

Have you received God's gifts into your life?

Have you been called by God?

If so, then these things are irrevocable, regardless of what hardship comes your way. I have personally found this to be true.

In 1984 I was badly treated at the start of my first imprisonment. I was almost beaten to death on numerous occasions and was kicked, punched and urinated on every day by the guards and other inmates. Every time the authorities interrogated me, they demanded to know the names of other house church leaders. I determined that I would not become a Judas, and I refused to answer any of their questions. I shut my mouth and decided it would be better to die than betray my coworkers, so I stopped eating and drinking and meditated on the Word of God. After a while the prisoners and the guards became amazed that I was still alive, for they knew that I had not had a thing to eat or drink for weeks. As my body perished, they placed bets on whether or not I would survive another night. The almighty God decided to preserve my life. He kept me alive for seventy-four days without food or water.

I have found, like Jonah, that when God has a call on our lives, He will never change His mind. Even if we run in the opposite direction, His call remains irrevocable. Even when I wanted to die, His call would not change! I believe God preserved me during this long fast simply because He wouldn't accept the offering of my life at that time. His plan for me was far from finished. He had more for me to do.

Brothers and sisters, when Jesus doesn't want your life to end, then it is completely impossible for you to die! He is in complete control. Historians say that the apostle John was lowered into a cauldron of boiling oil by the Emperor Domitian, but he miraculously survived. God had not finished with John. He still had to write the book of Revelation! Shadrach, Meshach and Abednego were thrown into a blazing furnace, but not a hair on their heads was singed because God's plan for these three young men was incomplete. Wicked men in China have tried to shoot believers, only for their guns to misfire again and again. Others have even survived hangings and attempts to throw them off cliffs or burn them alive.

If we could just catch a glimpse of how much our God is in control of this world and our lives, we would rest comfortably in His arms and would not be terrified by the daily news. Threats and intimidation would not cause our hearts to skip a single beat. Jesus is in control! He has declared, "All authority in heaven and on earth has been given to me" (Matt. 28:18). He assured the apostle John, "Do not be afraid. I am the First and the Last. I am the Living One; I was dead, and behold I am alive for ever and ever! And I hold the keys of death and

Hades" (Rev. 1:17–18). Jesus is also in control of what can occur in your life, for "what he opens no one can shut, and what he shuts no one can open" (Rev. 3:7).

My prayer for you is the same that Paul prayed for the Ephesians:

> I pray also that the eyes of your heart may be enlightened in order that you may know the hope to which he has called you, the riches of his glorious inheritance in the saints, and his incomparably great power for us who believe. That power is like the working of his mighty strength, which he exerted in Christ when he raised him from the dead and seated him at his right hand in the heavenly realms, far above all rule and authority, power and dominion, and every title that can be given, not only in the present age but also in the one to come. And God placed all things under his feet and appointed him to be head over everything for the church, which is his body, the fullness of him who fills everything in every way.
>
> Ephesians 1:18–23

God will never let His name be defamed. He will not allow someone to say, "God made a covenant with me, but He has not held up His end of the arrangement." The Lord's reputation is tied to His faithfulness in keeping His promises.

Did you ever wonder why God referred to Himself as the "God of Abraham, Isaac and Jacob" on many occasions throughout the Old Testament? Why didn't he include Moses or any of the other patriarchs in that list? After all, Jacob was labeled a "deceiver," while Moses is described as a "friend of God."

Watch carefully, for the answer is important.

Abraham (in Gen. 12:1–3), Isaac (26:2–5) and Jacob

(28:10–15) are the only three men God made a covenant with to make their descendants into a great nation that would bless the world! Every time God referred to Himself as the "God of Abraham, Isaac and Jacob," he was reminding the world of His covenants and His faithfulness. His very name and reputation were at stake among the nations, and the Lord will never allow His name to be defamed or His character tarnished. He is the almighty God of love, mercy and truth, and He always does what He promises to do.

The author of Hebrews explained that "when God made his promise to Abraham, since there was no one greater for him to swear by, he swore by himself, saying, 'I will surely bless you and give you many descendants.' And so after waiting patiently, Abraham received what was promised. Men swear by someone greater than themselves, and the oath confirms what is said and puts an end to all argument. Because God wanted to make the unchanging nature of his purpose very clear to the heirs of what was promised, he confirmed it with an oath. God did this so that, by two unchangeable things in which it is impossible for God to lie, we who have fled to take hold of the hope offered to us may be greatly encouraged" (Heb. 6:13–18).

When I was a teenager, Jesus called me to take the gospel to the South and West. At the time I thought this only meant that I should go to villages south and west of my own village near my home at Nanyang in Henan Province. Later my vision expanded and I realized God had called me to go to the provinces in the south and west of China. Years later, God called me to leave China, and I realized that the call He gave me back in 1974 was a worldwide call to take His Word and preach it around the globe. This call was a holy covenant between the Lord and me.

Just because you enter into a covenant with the Lord doesn't mean everything will be easy. On many occasions over the years, I have been arrested and tortured as I sought to obey God's call. My darkest moment was in 1997 when my legs were fractured and I lay in solitary confinement, with no hope of being released from prison. Rumors abounded that I would be executed, while others said I would face life in prison. In my despair I complained to the Lord and reminded Him of His call to me. I told Him, "When I was young You called me to preach Your gospel to the West and South. How can I do that now? I'm sitting here in this prison with crippled legs, and I'm resigned to rot here until the day I die. I'll never see my family again."

Faced with such a dim future, I grumbled and even accused the Lord, "Oh God, I just want to serve You and spread Your gospel, but now I'm stuck here in this cell and cannot even walk. You are weak and failed to protect me. You have cheated me!"

As the weeks slowly passed, I became more and more depressed at my situation. My wife, Deling, was in the women's prison, and I had no idea what had become of my two children. It seemed as if the Lord had rejected me and left me to rot in prison forever. My legs were crippled and my spirit crushed. Each night I propped my lame legs up against the wall to try to lessen the pain.

It was the lowest point of my life.

At that point, Jesus came to me and reaffirmed His covenant. He told me, "This prison is real, but I am the Truth!" This made all the difference, because Jesus promised, "The truth will set you free" (John 8:31). My Savior had not forgotten me, for it is impossible for Him to forsake one of His children! He spoke His Word to me and commanded me to get up and walk.

Nobody may know where you are, but this is not the truth. The truth is that Jesus will never leave or forsake you! Your body might be shackled to a wall, but this is not the truth. The truth is that Jesus and His Word can never be chained! Read what the apostle Paul wrote from prison: "Remember Jesus Christ, raised from the dead, descended from David. This is my gospel, for which I am suffering even to the point of being chained like a criminal. But God's word is not chained. Therefore I endure everything for the sake of the elect, that they too may obtain the salvation that is in Christ Jesus, with eternal glory" (2 Tim. 2:8–10).

By His great power and mercy, I walked out of the Zhengzhou Prison and continued to proclaim the gospel. God told me in a dream, "I will send you to a new place. You won't understand a single word of their language. There will be many strange faces before you, but you must obey My command: 'Go and awaken those people!' "

A short time later the Lord, through a brave brother, helped me to leave China, and ever since I have been preaching in the South and all around the Western world as the Lord had promised.

The God of covenants always keeps His promises! Sometimes we struggle to see Him through the storms of life, but the truth remains that "God is not a man, that he should lie, nor a son of man, that he should change his mind. Does he speak and then not act? Does he promise and not fulfill?" (Num. 23:19).

Back to our story: King Jehoshaphat and the people of Judah poured out their hearts to God. He encouraged them with these words: "Do not be afraid or discouraged because of this vast army. For the battle is not yours, but God's. Tomorrow march down against them. . . . You will not have to fight this battle. Take up your positions; stand firm and see the deliverance the LORD will give you, O Judah and Jerusalem. Do not be afraid; do not be discouraged. Go out to face them tomorrow, and the LORD will be with you" (2 Chron. 20:15–17).

When enemies surround you, remember that the battle belongs to the Lord. You are His child, and He will fight for you. Such dependence on God humbles us and causes us to praise Him. King Jehoshaphat "bowed with his face to the ground, and all the people of Judah and Jerusalem fell down in worship before the LORD. Then some Levites from the Kohathites and Korahites stood up and praised the LORD, the God of Israel, with very loud voice" (2 Chron. 20:18–19).

God brought about a great victory for Judah. He fought for His people, causing confusion to come upon the enemy so that they destroyed one another. The rout was so complete that "when the men of Judah came to the place that overlooks the desert and looked toward the vast army, they saw only dead bodies lying on the ground; no one had escaped. So Jehoshaphat and his men went to carry off their plunder, and they found among them a great amount of equipment and clothing and also articles of value – more than they could take away. There was so much plunder that it took three days to collect it" (2 Chron. 20:24–25).

Three days to collect all the plunder! Can you imagine it? When God fights on behalf of His people, the enemy stands no chance. We must realize that fighting in our own strength is futile, and we must cry out to God for help. The kingdom of God advances through weakness, not through human strength and activity. The Bible warns us about trusting in human power to achieve our goals. In one place it says, "Cursed is the one who trusts in man, who depends on flesh for his strength and whose heart turns away from the LORD" (Jer. 17:5).

The story of Jehoshaphat and the Edomites concludes with these beautiful words: "The fear of God came upon all the kingdoms of the countries when they heard how the LORD had fought against the enemies of Israel. And the kingdom of Jehoshaphat was at peace, for his God had given him rest on every side" (2 Chron. 20:29–30).

Such victories are experienced by those who diligently seek the God of covenants.

23

Working in God's Harvest

> A revival is no more a miracle than a crop of wheat....
> Revival occurs when you go to bed exhausted and wake
> up exhausted.
>
> *Charles G. Finney*

There should never be anyone without work to do in the kingdom of God. Paul told the Christians in Ephesus that doing good works for Jesus is the very reason God saved them: "For we are God's workmanship, created in Christ Jesus to do good works, which God prepared in advance for us to do" (Eph. 2:10).

Not only did God save you to do good works, but He has already prepared something specific for each person. This is good news. It means there is a task that God has uniquely gifted you for and called you to do. Our role is simply to take Jesus' hand and let Him lead us and reveal what He wants us to do. Indeed, God not only gives you the power to work for Him; He even gives you the desire to want to do so in the first place. Paul told the Philippians, "Continue to work out your salvation with fear and trembling, for it is God who works in you to will and to act according to his good purpose" (Phil. 2:12–13).

Many Christians are paralyzed with fear and inactivity. This is one of the major strategies of the Devil. First he tries to stop every person from becoming a child of God. Once it happens, however, he tries to ensure they won't be active in working in God's harvest field. No wonder the Lord said, "The harvest is plentiful, but the workers are few. Ask the Lord of the harvest, therefore, to send out workers into his harvest field" (Luke 10:2).

Many Christians today are deceived. Somehow they think that being saved means they can sit back and enjoy the Lord and do nothing else while they wait for Him to come again. This attitude is so strange to me that I find it astonishing. In China all the Christians I know are busy working for the Lord, preaching the gospel to people nearby and those far away, teaching and encouraging the saints and generally doing all they can to advance the kingdom of God.

In China every believer is an evangelist. That is why so many millions of people have become Christians, with millions more being added to God's kingdom every year. Among the house churches, evangelists sometimes return from preaching in faraway places and greet one another by asking, "How many people have you led to the Lord *today*?" Many Christians lead people to Jesus every single day. Some refuse to go to sleep until they have witnessed for the Lord and had the opportunity of bringing lost sheep into His fold. They want to be like one of those mentioned in the Bible, which declares, "Those who are wise will shine like the brightness of the heavens, and those who lead many to righteousness, like the stars for ever and ever" (Dan. 12:3).

During my lifetime I believe China will become a truly Christian nation, with the gospel thoroughly saturating every segment of society. In some areas we are already beginning to see this happen. China is not being transformed for Jesus because we sit around thinking and talking about God's work. No! We invest all our energy, time and resources in reaching the lost. The church prays hard and works hard for the Lord. Many thousands of Christians have willingly endured brutal treatment and imprisonment in order to see the vision of a redeemed China become a reality.

In 1982 the house churches in my home province of Henan decided to send a team of seventeen evangelists to eastern Sichuan Province. After arriving, they spread out to different counties. In the first month God did many wonderful works and revival broke out. The local authorities were furious to find the gospel being proclaimed in their area and initiated a severe crackdown. Thirteen of the evangelists were arrested, badly beaten and sent back to Henan.

One of the evangelists, Brother Wang, managed to escape. He hurried back to Henan, alerted the church to the arrests and described the brutal beatings each member of the team had received. Many had suffered broken bones. When a group of five local believers went to the train station to welcome the injured evangelists home, they were arrested and cruelly beaten at the police station. Their heads were smashed, and bruises covered every part of their bodies. The police tied them up in an inhumane manner and subjected them to additional abuses with dreaded electric batons.

The Christians didn't harbor any resentment or bitterness towards their persecutors at all. Indeed, they thanked God for the great privilege of partaking in the "fellowship of sharing in his sufferings" (Phil. 3:10). They rejoiced "because they had been counted worthy of suffering disgrace for the Name" (Acts 5:41).

They felt sorry for the men who had carried out these tortures, and prayed fervently for them.

When the believers in Henan heard that so many evangelists had been arrested and severely injured, many immediately volunteered to go to Sichuan in their place. These replacement evangelists were also arrested and sent back to Henan covered in their own blood and bruises. The response of the church was to send yet more workers. Finally, after much suffering, there was a spiritual breakthrough and a strong body of believers emerged in eastern Sichuan. Revival broke out in several areas, and today there are tens of thousands of Christians where there had previously been none.

The sacrifice was worth it.

If nobody had gone to Sichuan with the gospel, the people there would still be lost in their sin and hopelessness. Revival doesn't come about by sitting around hoping for something to happen! Don't expect a cloud from heaven to float down one day and lots of people to kneel down and repent of their sins. Revival comes when blood-bought disciples decide to give their past, present and future to do whatever it takes to proclaim the good news! The Bible states the obvious by asking, "How, then, can they call on the one they have not believed in? And how can they believe in the one of whom they have not heard? And how can they hear without someone preaching to them? And how can they preach unless they are sent?" (Rom. 10:14–15).

The apostle Paul also saw great revival in his ministry everywhere he went. Did this come simply by a sovereign move of the Holy Spirit, carrying Paul along on a blissful journey? In comparing himself to other apostles, Paul told the Corinthians, "I worked harder than all of them—yet not I, but the grace of God that was with me" (1 Cor. 15:10).

Later, the great apostle summarized some of the troubles he had faced in his ministry. Notice how many times the word "danger" appears in this one passage. He said:

I have worked much harder, been in prison more frequently, been flogged more severely, and been exposed to death again and again. Five times I received from the Jews the forty lashes minus one. Three times I was beaten with rods, once I was stoned, three times I was shipwrecked, I spent a night and a day in the open sea, I have been constantly on the move. I have been in danger from rivers, in danger from bandits, in danger from my own countrymen, in danger from Gentiles; in danger in the city, in danger in the country, in danger at sea; and in danger from false brothers. I have labored and toiled and have often gone without sleep; I have known hunger and thirst and have often gone without food; I have been cold and naked. Besides everything else, I face daily the pressure of my concern for all the churches.

2 Corinthians 11:23–28

Paul spared no effort in serving Christ, and he knew what hard work was. It seems an overemphasis has been put on grace in the Western church, so that believers are lulled into thinking their job is to lie down and do nothing for God. I cherish God's grace, make no mistake about that, but experiencing His grace is meant to produce just the opposite effect in our lives. His grace should motivate and empower us to serve Jesus and to make Him known everywhere!

If you claim to have faith in Jesus, then you can prove it by showing us your deeds. When you stand before the judgment seat of Christ, do you expect to be judged according to "your heart"? Is this biblical?

In the parable of the sheep and goats, the Lord spoke about those people who will be welcomed into heaven and those who will be banished to hell. First, let's look at those who were welcomed into heaven: "Then the King will say to those on his right, 'Come, you who are blessed by my Father; take your inheritance, the kingdom prepared for you since the creation of the world. For I was hungry and you gave me something to eat, I was thirsty and you gave me something to drink, I was a stranger and you invited me in, I needed clothes and you clothed me, I was sick and you looked after me, I was in prison and you came to visit me'" (Matt. 25:34–36).

Conversely, Jesus taught:

> *"Then he will say to those on his left, 'Depart from me, you who are cursed, into the eternal fire prepared for the devil and his angels. For I was hungry and you gave me nothing to eat, I was thirsty and you gave me nothing to drink, I was a stranger and you did not invite me in, I needed clothes and you did not clothe me, I was sick and in prison and you did not look after me.' They also will answer, 'Lord, when did we see you hungry or thirsty or a stranger or needing clothes or sick or in prison, and did not help you?' He will reply, 'I tell you the truth, whatever you did not do for one of the least of these, you did not do for me.' Then they will go away to eternal punishment, but the righteous to eternal life."*
>
> *Matthew 25:41–46*

From these verses you will have no doubt noticed that our deeds are important to God. In this parable, people's eternal destination depended on the fruit of their lives that was expressed through their actions. What mattered here was what they had *done*. Jesus taught that you can't claim to know God yet do nothing to serve Him.

Let's also read what Jesus said to the churches in the book of Revelation. He didn't tell the Sardinians that He knew their hearts. Rather, He told them, "I know your deeds.... I have not found your deeds complete in the sight of my God" (Rev. 3:1–2). To the Laodiceans He said, "I know your deeds, that you are neither cold nor hot. I wish you were either one or the other!" (Rev. 3:15). The Ephesians were similarly told, "I know your deeds, your hard work and your perseverance" (Rev. 2:2), while to the church in Thyatira our risen Lord said, "I know your deeds, your love and faith, your service and perseverance, and that you are now doing more than you did at first" (Rev. 2:19).

Did you catch the key phrases?

"Deeds," "hard work," "perseverance," "doing more than you did at first" ...

Jesus doesn't expect you to sit on your backside for the rest of your life while you try to perfect your doctrine. Rather, He wants you to get busy in His harvest field, sharing the life of Jesus with those who know nothing about Him.

Does this mean that we can get into heaven solely by performing good deeds?

Of course not!

People will only get into heaven by being born again, and in so doing becoming children of God. It is only by the blood of our precious Lord Jesus that our sins are forgiven and we are restored to right relationship with our heavenly Father.

However, if you really *have* been born again, the evidence

that your faith is genuine is demonstrated by whether or not you have gone and borne good fruit for the kingdom of God. If you really know God, you will be serving His purposes and working for His kingdom. You won't be able to sit around while the world goes to hell.

Perhaps James stated it most clearly for us: "What good is it, my brothers, if a man claims to have faith but has no deeds? Can such faith save him? Suppose a brother or sister is without clothes and daily food. If one of you says to him, 'Go, I wish you well; keep warm and well fed,' but does nothing about his physical needs, what good is it? In the same way, faith by itself, if it is not accompanied by action, is dead. But someone will say, 'You have faith; I have deeds.' Show me your faith without deeds, and I will show you my faith by what I do. You believe that there is one God. Good! Even the demons believe that – and shudder. You foolish man, do you want evidence that faith without deeds is useless? … You see that a person is justified by what he does and not by faith alone" (James 2:14–20, 24).

When a person first comes to faith in Jesus Christ and is radically transformed, that person is overcome with joy and can't wait to tell his family and friends about his experiences. Such a person does not have to force himself to do this, for it is the most natural thing in the world. The desire to serve God is not something a Christian has to conjure up in his own strength. If a person escapes from a burning house, will he not do all he can to help those still trapped inside?

Have you ever felt you would die unless you shared the goodness of Jesus Christ with others? If not, it is time to kneel down and ask God to give you a fresh revelation of the joy and presence of the Lord. If you are truly saved, then you will be a witness for Jesus Christ and you will naturally bear good fruit for God's kingdom.

During the time of the prophet Elisha, an enemy army besieged Samaria, trapping the people inside the city walls. A huge number of Aramean soldiers camped outside the city, waiting to massacre all of the inhabitants. Before long the besieged people of Samaria were starving. Things became so bad that one child was boiled and eaten by his mother and another woman just so they could survive (see 2 Kings 6:24–33). In their desperation, the besieged people cried out to the Lord for help. God performed a great miracle by sending a spirit of confusion into the enemy camp, causing the soldiers to flee into the night.

The captives inside the city wall were unaware of what had happened. God chose four lepers, considered the lowest part of society, to break the news. These men walked into the Aramean camp and entered a deserted tent. They "ate and drank, and carried away silver, gold and clothes, and went off and hid them. They returned and entered another tent and took some things from it and hid them also" (2 Kings 7:8).

This is how many Christians are today. They are happy to receive God's blessings and store them up, but they have become so absorbed in the blessings that they are blind to God's purposes. The four lepers thankfully came to their senses and realized it was a sin to keep all these good things to themselves while their countrymen perished inside the city walls. They said to each other, "We're not doing right. This is a day of good news and we are keeping it to ourselves. If we wait until daylight, punishment will overtake us. Let's go at once and report this to the royal palace" (2 Kings 7:9).

Brothers and sisters, today *is* a day of good news!

Are you keeping it to yourself?

The gospel is a message not only of faith and grace, but also of action and work.

As you step out and begin to work for the kingdom of God, there will be times where you need a time of rest and refreshment so that you will be ready for more action. For those who feel like giving up, the Bible gives the following encouragement: "Let us not become weary in doing good, for at the proper time we will reap a harvest if we do not give up. Therefore, as we have opportunity, let us do good to all people, especially to those who belong to the family of believers" (Gal. 6:9–10).

Let's not fool ourselves; one day our works will be judged by God. It would be terrible to stand before Him with nothing to show for the abundant grace He has lavished on us. Don't just sit around thinking and talking about serving the Lord. Go out and do it! If you wait until you are perfect, then you will be waiting your whole life.

It will be too late for excuses when we stand before the judgment seat of Christ. It won't work to claim we didn't know how desperate the world was to hear about God's salvation, only for us to turn our backs and ignore them. The Bible is very clear for those who plead ignorance: "Rescue those being led away to death; hold back those staggering toward slaughter. If you say, 'But we knew nothing about this,' does not he who weighs the heart perceive it? Does not he who guards your life know it? Will he not repay each person according to what he has done?" (Prov. 24:11–12).

Don't think you need to be some great preacher or have theological training to share the gospel! To be a preacher, all you have to do is obey Jesus. Simply share those things from God's Word that He has placed in your heart. If you can tell another person about what Jesus Christ has done in your life, you will be surprised how interested they are. Most people have no interest in arguing theology, but when someone they know sincerely and respectfully shares their experiences, they will listen.

Your testimony is a powerful weapon! Don't underestimate it. In speaking of the saints' victory over Satan, the Bible says, "They overcame him by the blood of the Lamb and by the word of their testimony; they did not love their lives so much as to shrink from death" (Rev. 12:11).

Next, ask God to give you a worldwide vision. God wants to reach the whole world, and you should too. Many churches today only focus on reaching their local communities. It is good to reach your local community, but you should do this at the same time you are reaching the nations of the world. Jesus commanded the apostles to preach the gospel in Jerusalem, Judea, Samaria and to the uttermost ends of the earth. He didn't mean we should do one at a time, but that both our home area and the ends of the earth should be reached simultaneously.

Remember that you have been saved to do good works, which God has prepared in advance for you to do (Eph. 2:10), so pray and ask God to unfold His plan for your life. Ask God to bring you into fellowship with other Christians who have a burning desire to serve Him and reach the world. It is necessary to walk into battle with others rather than by yourself. Ask the Holy Spirit to show you what is on His heart. As He does, be obedient and do whatever He tells you, and go wherever He sends you. There is so much to do in this world that you will never lack for work.

Whatever you do, don't put conditions on God. Don't say,

"Lord, I am willing to do this and that, but I refuse to cooperate if you want me to do anything outside of this criteria." Some people are so rigid in their plans that if God tells them to go somewhere but the dates fall on their scheduled annual holiday, they will tell the Lord He must have got it wrong! If you are a follower of Jesus Christ, you have no right to put any conditions on God. "You are not your own; you were bought at a price. Therefore honor God with your body" (1 Cor. 6:19–20).

Does your life *really* belong to God or to yourself? Is He the Lord of your life, or are you still clinging to control, setting your own schedule and fitting God into your busy agenda wherever you are able?

God knows how to best use your life to glorify Him. He knows the special gifts He has given you and where you can be most effective for His kingdom. Will you obey our Lord and "go into all the world and preach the good news to all creation" (Mark 16:15)? His command was not just for the disciples, but for every follower throughout the world in every generation. He did not *ask* His followers to go; He *commanded* us!

Are you willing to give your life to reach AIDS sufferers in Africa or slum-dwellers in India? Would you say, "Yes, Lord," if He calls you to reach businessmen in the Middle East?

Let's get busy for the Lord Jesus! Realize of course that you cannot work for your salvation, for salvation is only by grace and faith. Our work for Jesus must be the result of an overflow of our relationship with Him. But once you realize that you are saved, surely it is time to get busy for the Lord, making Him known to as many people as possible.

Jesus is worth giving your very best to. He was willing to

reach down and die for you. Are we willing to obey the Great Commission in return?

There is no time to waste. Your days on this earth are few and precious, and it's time to kneel down *now* and make a commitment to God that you will not waste any more time. Ask the Lord of the harvest to show you how to proceed, and He surely will.

24

Bondage and Freedom

> It is for freedom that Christ has set us free. Stand firm, then, and do not let yourselves be burdened again by a yoke of slavery.
>
> *Galatians 5:1*

> The Spirit of the Sovereign LORD is on me, because the LORD has anointed me to preach good news to the poor. He has sent me to bind up the brokenhearted, to proclaim freedom for the captives and release from darkness for the prisoners.
>
> *Isaiah 61:1*

As a servant of the Lord, I have been called to follow the example of Jesus to proclaim the good news, to heal the sick and those in despair and to proclaim freedom for those who are spiritually bound. I have found that perhaps the saddest person in the world is a Christian who has experienced the joy of being set free by Jesus Christ, only to allow himself to slip back into bondage and slavery. Tragically, such Christians can be found in the millions, all around the world.

Freedom is the main subject of Paul's letter to the Galatians.

The church there had been birthed in great power. Men and women were set free from the prisons of their sin and disobedience, and great joy and peace were experienced. Over the course of time, however, the Galatians allowed themselves to be dominated by legalism. Satan deceived them into thinking that although their initial salvation was totally dependent upon God's grace and mercy, now their Christian lives had to be lived out in their own strength.

The great apostle wrote to them in a very direct manner:

> *You foolish Galatians! Who has bewitched you? Before your very eyes Jesus Christ was clearly portrayed as crucified. I would like to learn just one thing from you: Did you receive the Spirit by observing the law, or by believing what you heard? Are you so foolish? After beginning with the Spirit, are you now trying to attain your goal by human effort? Have you suffered so much for nothing—if it really was for nothing? Does God give you his Spirit and work miracles among you because you observe the law, or because you believe what you heard?*
>
> Galatians 3:1–5

How about you, my beloved friend?

Have you started your Christian life with the Spirit but are now trying to live for Christ through your own efforts?

If you are a preacher or pastor, have you lost your way so that your "ministry" no longer contains a flow of fresh living water? Do you offer the flock dry morsels that they struggle to digest and that have no nutritional value? If so, it is possible you have "lost connection with the Head, from whom the whole body, supported and held together by its ligaments and sinews, grows as God causes it to grow" (Col. 2:19).

The good news is that Jesus loves His bride, and He will come to the rescue! If your Christian life has been disconnected from the living water that flows from close communion with the Father, there is hope for you. There is always hope for the person who repents and starts walking in the direction ordained by the Lord. If you have experienced Christ's salvation, then it is time to "set your hearts on things above, where Christ is seated at the right hand of God. Set your minds on things above, not on earthly things. For you died, and your life is now hidden with Christ in God. When Christ, who is your life, appears, then you also will appear with him in glory" (Col. 3:1–4).

In 1949 the Communists came to power in China, and within a few years everything started to change for the church. Initial harassment turned into discrimination, and discrimination soon became full-blown persecution. The professional clergy was blown away in the storm. Thousands of pastors and priests were sent to prison, where they faced years of bitter struggle. Many stayed true to their faith, but others gave up and fell away under pressure.

By the mid–1970s the church in China had been stripped of everything we had previously held on to. All religious props were demolished. We had no pastors, no church buildings and no Bibles or hymnals.

All we had was Jesus.

We later realized that God had allowed the terrible persecution in our country because He wanted to rebuild His church in a way that would make us capable of bringing glory to Jesus. He desired to equip us so we would successfully reach the one billion lost souls in China. The Lord knew that the existing structures had to first be completely demolished.

It was an excruciatingly painful time for countless saints, but when the body of Christ started to re-emerge from the wilderness, we had been transformed. The furnace of affliction had purified the church and revealed the gold of Jesus within. Where there had once been much selfish ambition and pride, there was now brokenness and humility. Where the believers had formerly relied on professional preachers to do all the work, there was now a kingdom of priests to serve our God. Before there had been paid evangelists whose job it was to spread the gospel. Now all believers were evangelists, and every street became a pulpit.

We experienced God's presence and power in a mighty way, and the continuing persecution allowed us to remain focused on the Lord.

In some churches I have visited around the world, the pastors and leaders have somehow been deluded into thinking their role is to control and dominate the flock. They fear any potential loss of power and authority and swiftly crack down on any activity or initiative that doesn't originate with them.

I have also visited many Christian ministries where the president of the ministry operates just like a prison warden. He exerts control and makes sure everyone toes the line. These various churches and ministries have become like huge prisons, capturing and keeping people locked away from the freedom they have in Christ. Nobody is allowed to do anything outside of the rules, just as a warden ensures that all inmates submit to the prison rules and stay inside the walls. They use various ways to capture people into their churches, denominations and organizations and then invent creative strategies to seal them off from the rest of the world. From that moment on, instead of being "kingdom-minded" Christians who seek first the kingdom of God, these captives are forced to expend all their energies on servicing the infrastructure of that organization to ensure its ongoing survival.

In the name of Jesus Christ, I declare that all such walls will be torn down so that those who have been pushed down and oppressed will be free! Anyplace where people are surrounded by walls and tightly controlled by others is a prison. The Chinese character for "prisoner" is a person who is enclosed within a square. Tragically, many Christians today are prisoners inside churches and organizations that seek to control their lives. To such people the Christian faith has become a dreary chore of obeying man-made rules and submitting to ungodly structures. To such prisoners I want to proclaim the good news that Jesus Christ can set you free!

Such organizations and churches have little blessing of God in their midst, even though they may be experts at convincing others that they do. God hates it when self-seeking people exert spiritual control over others.

He especially hates it when it is done in His name!

If you are a pastor or in some position of church leadership, carefully examine your heart and motives and ask God to transform you so that you become the kind of shepherd God desires. It is a fearful thing to offend God in such a way. All church leaders should kneel down and prayerfully read the scriptural warnings for those who shepherd God's flock. Let's look at chapter 34 of Ezekiel for example:

> *The word of the LORD came to me: "Son of man, prophesy against the shepherds of Israel; prophesy and say to them: 'This is what the Sovereign LORD says: Woe to the shepherds of Israel who only take care of themselves! Should not shepherds*

take care of the flock? You eat the curds, clothe yourselves with the wool and slaughter the choice animals, but you do not take care of the flock. You have not strengthened the weak or healed the sick or bound up the injured. You have not brought back the strays or searched for the lost. You have ruled them harshly and brutally. So they were scattered because there was no shepherd, and when they were scattered they became food for all the wild animals. My sheep wandered over all the mountains and on every high hill. They were scattered over the whole earth, and no one searched or looked for them.

"'Therefore, you shepherds, hear the word of the LORD: ... This is what the Sovereign LORD says: I am against the shepherds and will hold them accountable for my flock. I will remove them from tending the flock so that the shepherds can no longer feed themselves. I will rescue my flock from their mouths, and it will no longer be food for them.'"

Ezekiel 34:1–7, 10

On many occasions I have been asked if I think persecution will come to the Western church. My answer might surprise you. I believe that if you find yourself enslaved inside a controlling church structure of legalism and bondage, then you are already being persecuted! So many Christians seem impossibly distracted from hearing God's voice. Instead of listening to that still, small voice that brings true peace and joy, they blindly follow the voices of mainstream religion. The worst kind of persecution for a Christian is when you are separated from the joy and presence of the Holy Spirit.

When your ability to hear and obey the voice of the Holy Spirit stops, you tend to believe a self-serving gospel that leads to a false sense of security. Over time, you start to compromise and ignore sin in your life. Such believers eventually lose sight of their need of Jesus. This is the definition of a backslidden Christian, and millions are in this place today.

My friend, if the wonderful freedom and vibrancy you once experienced in Christ have been replaced by bondage, I assure you there is hope. The hope for you is found in the cross of Christ.

The cross is not a piece of jewelry to wear around your neck. Nor is it two clean pieces of intersecting timber placed on the wall of your church. The cross of Christ is soaked in blood and pain. If you take up your cross and follow Him, your life too will be soaked in blood and pain. This has been our experience in China, and the cross has delivered us from bondage and enabled us to walk in wonderful freedom. The gospel you have heard all these years – that Christianity will bring comfort and pleasant experiences to your life – is a false gospel. Paul warned the Galatians, "I am astonished that you are so quickly deserting the one who called you by the grace of Christ and are turning to a different gospel – which is really no gospel at all" (Gal. 1:6–7).

You need to take up your cross, feel its weight on your shoulders and back, and start following Jesus every day. You may find your walk takes you out from under the false security of the prevailing church structures. You will find that others turn against you and criticize you on your journey, for many don't see the need to change. When these things happen, don't be alarmed, for Jesus has promised, "In this world you will have trouble. But take heart! I have overcome the world" (John 16:33).

As you follow Jesus, you will be attacked and maybe even killed for your faith. If you die, don't worry. Everyone has to die one day. You will just be following in the footsteps of our Lord.

Keep following Jesus, and let Him be your best friend. As you continue on your journey, you will find the chains that have bound you for so long will loosen and drop off one by one, and you will be free! Brothers and sisters, by God's grace and power I plan to continue to preach about God's wonderful acts and to testify to the truth of the Word of God.

Please lift up your head, and let our Lord give you strength and boldness to fearlessly declare the good news, for "the Lord is the Spirit, and where the Spirit of the Lord is, there is freedom. And we, who with unveiled faces all reflect the Lord's glory, are being transformed into his likeness with ever-increasing glory" (2 Cor. 3:17–18).

25

A New Wineskin

He told them this parable: "No one tears a patch from a new garment and sews it on an old one. If he does, he will have torn the new garment, and the patch from the new will not match the old. And no one pours new wine into old wineskins. If he does, the new wine will burst the skins, the wine will run out and the wineskins will be ruined. No, new wine must be poured into new wineskins."

Luke 5:36–38

Usually when Christians speak about our needing more of the Holy Spirit's transforming power in our lives, and more miracles, few of us get upset. We all want to drink in the good wine of the Lord, and all except the most hard-hearted of believers acknowledge that they need Jesus in a fresh way.

I have a message to share with you, however, that is much less popular in Christian circles today. Some are so uncomfortable with what I am about to share that they will label it heresy. My invitation to you is to weigh my words with the Scriptures, and judge it for yourself.

I need to share this message because we can talk all we want about the wine of the Lord in our lives, but it will be of little value unless our wineskins are able to contain the wine. When Jesus talked about this, I believe He was talking not only about our lives as being the wineskin, but also, in a broader sense, about the church as being the wineskin.

Since coming out of China in 1997, I have been invited to speak in many hundreds of churches around the world, from huge meetings in megachurches in the United States, to tiny groups that meet in homes. I have been invited to share God's Word in prisons, hospitals, caves, tents and cathedrals in places as diverse as the Middle East, Australia and New Zealand, all throughout Europe, Russia, North and South Asia, the Americas, parts of Africa and even the remote Pacific island of Tahiti.

In all these places I have been blessed to meet many wonderful disciples of Jesus Christ, and I have been thrilled to see the faces of so many fellow pilgrims on this journey for the Lord.

At the same time, I have gained a growing concern for the wineskin, the church, in many places. To be honest, I believe that in their current condition and structure, many churches (the wineskin) are unable to contain the presence of the Holy Spirit (the wine). This is demonstrated when zealous young believers, full of fire from heaven's altar, are placed in the prevailing church structures. Within a short time their enthusiasm has been dampened down, and the spark of life and faith in them, which thrilled the heart of Jesus, is extinguished as they are forced to submit to systems of church life that are neither biblical nor helpful.

The whole structure of church life in some countries seems to be geared toward producing the opposite kind of Christian life from what Jesus demonstrated. Every time I am asked to speak at a Bible school or seminary, I tell the students that they need to get out of their chairs and go to the needy people in the streets outside. I always plead with the faculty of these institutions to train the students to go into the society and interact with people. Alas, almost all of these schools only seem interested in educating believers in how to exist inside of their church buildings.

God wants His children to be out among the streets and marketplaces of the world. He doesn't want His body to be a bunch of professional Christians whose only solution to people's problems is to invite them to come inside their church building on Sundays. Jesus didn't tell Zacchaeus, "I would like to invite you to an evangelistic campaign next week so you can hear my message." No! Jesus knew that Zacchaeus was a despised tax collector with many problems in his life. The Lord wanted to involve Himself directly in this man's family and called out, " 'Zacchaeus, come down immediately. I must stay at your house today.' So he came down at once and welcomed him gladly" (Luke 19:5–6).

Jesus was never afraid to spend time with sinners. In fact, "when the teachers of the law who were Pharisees saw him eating with the 'sinners' and tax collectors, they asked his disciples: 'Why does he eat with tax collectors and "sinners"?' On hearing this, Jesus said to them, 'It is not the healthy who need a doctor, but the sick. I have not come to call the righteous, but sinners' " (Mark 2:16–17). Don't become so "holy" that you fear being contaminated by contact with those outside of the church. Jesus went for dinner at the home of Zacchaeus because He knew this man and his family desperately needed the heavenly Father's intervention in their messed-up lives.

There is always a conflict between Christians who desire to be beacons of light to the lost society around them and those who prefer to maintain a buffer zone between them and the "big bad world." How many people were offended when Jesus went into Zacchaeus's house? The Bible says, "All the people saw this and began to mutter, 'He has gone to be the guest of a "sinner"'" (Luke 19:7).

When Zacchaeus announced that he would give away half his possessions to the poor, Jesus didn't say, "About time, Zacchaeus! After all, you have cheated people for years with your exorbitant taxes." Instead, Jesus rejoiced that this man had opened his heart to God, and He announced, "Today salvation has come to this house, because this man, too, is a son of Abraham. For the Son of Man came to seek and to save what was lost" (Luke 19:9–10).

How would your fellowship receive a Zacchaeus? He was considered the scum of society, maybe like a pimp or a drug addict today. Would you shy away from him and think that such a wicked man could not possibly be saved? Or would you be like Jesus, willing to spend time with him and his family so that they could change and become sons and daughters of God? May the Lord put a kingdom heart in all of us so that we will be servants who march forward in grace, love and power.

Centuries ago Christians built remote monasteries in the mountains to help them get away from people and supposedly avoid the "contamination" of the world. Today in Protestant circles the same thinking prevails in a different guise. It results in a stream of believers only equipped to play spiritual games inside the safety of their church walls, but totally ill prepared when they have to leave their Christian environment and interact with real people in the outside world. This is tragic. Some nations are perishing without a viable gospel witness, while many Christians lock themselves away. Such an insular kind of Christianity is very dangerous for those who practice it. Take note of the words of Jesus: "You are the salt of the earth. But if the salt loses its saltiness, how can it be made salty again? It is no longer good for anything, except to be thrown out and trampled by men. You are the light of the world. A city on a hill cannot be hidden. Neither do people light a lamp and put it under a bowl. Instead they put it on its stand, and it gives light to everyone in the house. In the same way, let your light shine before men, that they may see your good deeds and praise your Father in heaven" (Matt. 5:13–16).

Many Christians pray for revival to come to their nation, but few are willing to be the salt and light to their communities like Jesus was. I have been invited to many churches in Europe in recent years, and I have been clearly telling the believers, "You should be ashamed because you have heard the gospel thousands of times and have heard about His healing power. But because you don't believe it, you don't experience it, and you are becoming more and more spiritually sick by the day." I have also bluntly told the leaders of these churches, "For centuries you have been busy constructing expensive church buildings, but now there are fewer and fewer people coming to them. Something must have gone totally wrong."

What has gone wrong is that Satan has deceived the church leaders in Europe and many other parts of the world, so that over time Christianity became something to be practiced inside a building instead of being a pulsating, life-transforming encounter with the living God that spills over and impacts the unsaved world. Christians have stopped having true faith in Jesus and have learned to rely on their pastors or priests.

258 | Living Water

Unless the Western church returns to biblical roots, it will continue its downward slide to irrelevance and oblivion.

I was quite discouraged when I shared this message at a meeting in Germany recently, because I could see that as my words entered into the minds of the listeners, they started to think about it and analyze it, and then they became totally lost in their thoughts. They could hardly open their mouths to pray because they did not believe a word of what I said. They don't understand that Jesus will not tolerate a dead church for long, for the church is meant to represent His kingdom to the lost people of the world. He is warning all such churches today: "Remember the height from which you have fallen! Repent and do the things you did at first. If you do not repent, I will come to you and remove your lampstand from its place" (Rev. 2:5).

One of the key areas in which the wineskin must be changed before the wine of the Holy Spirit can flow into your churches is the role of church leadership.

Jesus never intended one or two individuals to rule over His people. In fact, when James and John approached the Lord and asked for the right to sit next to His throne in heaven, Jesus sternly told them, "You know that the rulers of the Gentiles lord it over them, and their high officials exercise authority over them. Not so with you. Instead, whoever wants to become great among you must be your servant, and whoever wants to be first must be your slave—just as the Son of Man did not come to be served, but to serve, and to give his life as a ransom for many" (Matt. 20:25–28).

Jesus declared that among His people things must be done differently from the way they are done in the world system. In the world, all leadership models—be they political, social or professional—are based on a hierarchical model, with power flowing from the top down. This allows people in authority to "lord it over" others. Jesus told His disciples, "Not so with you." In His kingdom, all citizens are equal and no one person is permitted to exert control over another. Certainly there will be individuals with particular spiritual gifts and leadership abilities who will find themselves with different responsibilities from others, but they must fulfill their duties with gentleness and humility, being a servant to all and not "lording it over" others.

This fallen world system in which we live knows nothing about servant leaders. Rather, many leaders crave control and authority over other people, and they use people to reach their selfish aims and satisfy their prideful cravings. The world says, "Put your own interests first," but among God's children we should "do nothing out of selfish ambition or vain conceit, but in humility consider others better than [yourselves]" (Phil. 2:3).

Unfortunately, the spirit of the world has crept into the church as well, and millions of believers are controlled and dominated by manipulative shepherds, most of whom do not even realize they are doing it.

The Old Testament model of leadership is often followed by churches today. In the Old Testament we read of kings, prophets, judges and priests, whose job it was to represent God to the common people and to represent the people to God. The high priest had the most important and scariest responsibility of all—to enter into the presence of God in the Most Holy Place once a year. Nobody else had such access to God. They had to stay at a safe distance.

In the New Testament, however, the whole landscape changed forever! Jesus came to replace the Old Testament model and open up access to the Father through His blood.

Now *all* who put their faith in Christ are able to come into the Most Holy Place! What a dramatic change!

The exact moment when this change took place is recorded in the Scriptures: "When Jesus had cried out again in a loud voice, he gave up his spirit. At that moment the curtain of the temple was torn in two from top to bottom. The earth shook and the rocks split" (Matt. 27:50–51).

Have you ever thought about the significance of this event?

The thick curtain, which separated people from God, was torn in two! Now all who put their faith in the Son of God could freely come into the Father's presence without fear of punishment. For the first time in history since the garden of Eden, men and women could "approach the throne of grace with confidence, so that we may receive mercy and find grace to help us in our time of need" (Heb. 4:16).

The apostle Paul explained it this way: "Therefore, since we have been justified through faith, we have peace with God through our Lord Jesus Christ, through whom we have gained access by faith into this grace in which we now stand" (Rom. 5:1–2).

When Jesus died on the cross, He dismantled the hierarchical form of spiritual leadership. There is no need for formal, institutional kings and priests in the body of Christ anymore. Now Jesus "has made us to be a kingdom and priests to serve his God and Father" (Rev. 1:6).

This doesn't mean the body of Christ should just run amok, for there are clear New Testament teachings about elders who are given the responsibility to watch over the well-being of the flock, of deacons, apostles, teachers and so on. But these should not be considered *positions of office* as much as *calls of service* to God's people.

There is a world of difference.

As children of God, we are not called to have another person *over* us, for we are all equal in the sight of God, and He is over all. Today all believers are "sons of God through faith in Christ Jesus, for all of you who were baptized into Christ have clothed yourselves with Christ. There is neither Jew nor Greek, slave nor free, male nor female, for you are all one in Christ Jesus" (Gal. 3:26–28).

We must first submit to God. He is rightfully our King and Lord, and we have become His treasured possession. He paid for us by dying a gruesome death. Second, we are called to "submit to one another out of reverence for Christ" (Eph. 5:21). This includes wives being called to submit to their husbands, and husbands being commanded to love their wives as Christ loves the church. Such mutual, reverential submission in the body of Christ is designed to break the worldly cycle of people "lording it over" one another.

Unfortunately, the controlling style of leadership continues in thousands of churches today. God is angered by this, because people are usurping a position that God intended for Himself, and in many cases the flock that He died for is stunted in its spiritual growth and well-being because the sheep are forced into a sick system of spiritual domination and manipulation.

If you are a pastor, I encourage you to break free from what you have been taught at seminary and honestly examine the New Testament Scriptures afresh. Make sure you are not assuming a role that is unsupported by the Word of God.

One of the most poisonous influences on many of God's people today is that they are not allowed to actively participate in the body of Christ. Millions of sheep are told to sit in pews each Sunday and listen to speeches made by professional clergy. As each week passes, the listeners become more and more entrenched in their pews, and the pastors end up performing Old Testament roles that are no longer valid. If they are not careful, pastors can slip into a role in which they become mediators between God and the congregation. Some even claim that God only wants to speak to their congregations through them, because they are the leaders. This is Old Testament priesthood teaching, and it is killing the flock that Jesus paid the ultimate price for.

Pastor, the Lord has not called you to stand between God and His people. No! That is a very dangerous position to be in, for you are standing in the place of Jesus Christ. "For there is one God and one mediator between God and men, the man Christ Jesus, who gave himself as a ransom for all men" (1 Tim. 2:5–6).

Jesus wants to have a direct relationship with all of His children. He wants to teach them and walk with them, helping them to become the kind of wholehearted followers the Father is pleased with.

Perhaps the most dangerous dynamic in churches today is the division between the "clergy" and the "laity." This can lead to two separate classes among God's people – something that grieves the heart of the Father. Although most pastors and ministers I know are people who simply love God and seek to serve Him, a church dynamic may exist whereby leaders are elevated above other believers. This is a terrible path to tread. It results in the current proliferation of weak, spoon-fed believers who never or rarely lead anyone to faith in Christ. This dual class system in the church is reinforced every time the pastor ascends to a pulpit, positioned above the people. It is further re-inforced by the use of elevated titles such as "Reverend," "Pas-tor," "Bishop," and so on.

Jesus was very explicit in His teaching on this matter. After denouncing the teachers of the law and the Pharisees, He told the disciples, "But you are not to be called 'Rabbi,' for you have only one Master and you are all brothers. And do not call anyone on earth 'father,' for you have one Father, and he is in heaven. Nor are you to be called 'teacher,' for you have one Teacher, the Christ. The greatest among you will be your ser-vant. For whoever exalts himself will be humbled, and whoever humbles himself will be exalted" (Matt. 23:8–12).

No wonder so many churches today are spiritually bound! No wonder you don't see miracles like in the New Testament. Realizing the true presence of Jesus Christ is absent from their meetings, many churches try to artificially manufacture the life of the Holy Spirit through the use of loud and emotional music or a myriad of other techniques.

If you are a Christian worn down and exhausted by "church" life, I have good news for you! There are many parts of the world today where God has intervened, broken down the institutionalized church and placed it back in the hands of all believers.

In the West there is also an unhealthy dependence on church buildings. This fixation cannot be justified by any New Testament Scriptures. Billions of dollars are invested in the construction and maintenance of elaborate buildings, while comparatively very little is spent on worldwide evangelism and missions. There needs to be a huge shift away from the view of "church" as a building and back to the biblical view of "church" as simply a gathering of believers who come together to honor

God's Word and encourage one another. God is pleased with such a simple gathering, "for where two or three come together in my name, there am I with them" (Matt. 18:20).

It is not accurate to say we will "go" to church. Rather, we "are" the church! It is worth meditating on this fact for a while. From the moment Jesus died on the cross, God had no interest in dwelling in temples, tabernacles or any other buildings, but He wants to live within the very spirit of every person who trusts Jesus for eternal life. Paul said, "The God who made the world and everything in it is the Lord of heaven and earth and does not live in temples built by hands" (Acts 17:24). He further explained that "if the Spirit of him who raised Jesus from the dead is living in you, he who raised Christ from the dead will also give life to your mortal bodies through his Spirit, who lives in you" (Rom. 8:11).

Oh Lord, please give us a fresh revelation of Your indwelling presence! Grant us understanding to know "the mystery which has been hidden from ages and from generations, but now has been revealed to His saints ... which is Christ in you, the hope of glory" (Col. 1:26–27 NKJV).

In many nations around the world – including in the West – God is starting to break down centuries of man-made traditions and is reshaping His church the way He ordained it to be. Thousands of house churches are beginning to form, where sincere believers worship and seek the Lord together through His Word. Many Christians are experiencing true freedom for the first time as the oppressive chains of traditionalism are thrown off. They are discovering, to their amazement, that unbelievers who would never dream of setting foot inside a traditional church building are eager to learn about Jesus.

Not everyone is happy when God's people start to meet

together according to the New Testament pattern. The status quo runs very deep, and many have spent decades clothing themselves in the garments of tradition. Such teaching as I am sharing today makes them angry. They are comfortable in their pews, and they don't want to be stirred from their slumber. Others enjoy their positions of control and proudly believe they have a God-given right to continue to manipulate and abuse God's flock. They graduated from seminary, and they are paid a salary to mediate between God and men, or so they think. All talk of a new wineskin is dismissed, and those who thirst for a better way are often labeled "rebels".

For those who are frustrated because the wineskin is incapable of containing the new wine of God without bursting at the seams, I encourage you to obey the Word of God and meet together with other believers in a way that is consistent with the New Testament. I don't believe the setting is as important as the spiritual dynamic that operates in your meetings. There are many church services that have the presence of God, and many house church meetings where individuals have gained control over other believers. It is not the kind of building you meet in that is the issue, but the kind of system you are part of.

Do your leaders serve the other Christians, seeking to build them up?

Does everybody have an opportunity to actively participate in your gatherings, or are they dominated by one or two people who do almost all the singing, preaching and praying?

If you are serious about God and desire to be free to know Him more than ever before, then you may need to give serious thought to the wineskin you are part of. I don't tell you this to condemn you or anyone else. Rather, I share these things because God's heart is broken by the way so many of His children are bound by oppressive spiritual conditions. This also severely damages the witness Christians have among the culture and society in which they live.

Change is never easy, and in your pursuit for a biblical form of wineskin, you may pay a heavy price.

Many people have asked me why the church in China has experienced revival for so many years. Many sincere believers have asked, some with tears in their eyes, "Yun, what do we have to do to experience revival in our nation?"

The answer is not simple, because before the new wine can be poured, a new wineskin must be created. Otherwise "the new wine will burst the skins, the wine will run out and the wineskins will be ruined" (Luke 5:37).

The wineskin in its present form simply won't do.

26

The Wet Blanket Brigade

> "Blessed are you when people insult you, persecute you and falsely say all kinds of evil against you because of me. Rejoice and be glad, because great is your reward in heaven, for in the same way they persecuted the prophets who were before you."
>
> *Matthew 5:11–12*

I am called to be a servant of God, to preach the gospel and to be a faithful witness for God. I want to proclaim a message about the flaming gospel, for our Lord "makes his angels winds, his servants flames of fire" (Heb. 1:7).

In 2007 I was invited to speak at a revival meeting in Norway to celebrate the 100-year anniversary of the Azusa Street Revival in Los Angeles. Before I spoke, the Lord reminded me of a clear vision an elderly Christian man received at the time of the Los Angeles revival. In the vision he saw many rows of torches, all in a line, which formed a solid wall of fire.

As the fire of God burned brightly, a man with a wet blanket ran around trying to put out the flames, but his efforts were all to no avail. Every time he poured water onto the flames, the water had the effect of oil, strengthening the fire and causing the flames to burn more brightly.

Nobody can stop the fire of the Holy Spirit! The more people try to stop what God is doing, the more brightly the flames will burn. We have seen this in China during the past fifty years. The more persecution, imprisonment and hardship that have been thrown at the church, the stronger the revival fires have burned and the more people have been saved into God's kingdom. In China, "the kingdom of heaven has been forcefully advancing, and forceful men lay hold of it" (Matt. 11:12), and "the good news of the kingdom of God is being preached, and everyone is forcing his way into it" (Luke 16:16).

Do you know that our "God is a consuming fire" (Heb. 12:29)? He doesn't merely place a wall of fire around those who serve Him, but He *is* that wall of fire. Speaking of Jerusalem, God declared, "I myself will be a wall of fire around it ... and I will be its glory within" (Zech. 2:5).

Satan can't stand in the face of God's fire. He hates it and spends much time trying to douse the flames wherever the Holy Spirit has brought revival. The enemy is fighting a losing battle, however, as the fire of the gospel continues to spread throughout the earth. The more he tries to put the flames out with water, the more the Lord seems to be changing the water into fuel!

The enemy of our souls is a dirty fighter.
He attacks us in any way he can. He will attack you through your children, your health and your purity. He never sleeps and is looking for any foothold he can gain to diminish your testimony and degrade your life.

Satan's two main objectives in this world are to stop people from being saved and to try to distort and corrupt the church in order to reduce its effectiveness. The Devil cannot touch or hurt the Lord Jesus Christ, who is enthroned in heavenly glory. His victory is complete and sealed for all eternity. Instead, the Devil tries to destroy Christ's bride.

There are many churchgoers who see it as their duty to extinguish any sign of a fire in the church. Even the smell of a smoldering ember causes them great alarm. Often when a Christian gets a vision from God, "respectable and mature" believers come along and do everything they can to throw a wet blanket over the zealous disciple. Wet blankets are highly effective at dousing flames.

After quoting Scriptures like "God is a God of order," they advise the young zealot to calm down, return to the pew and submit to the teaching every Sunday morning. After a number of years of faithful attendance, he might be ready to attend seminary, where every last drop of enthusiasm for Jesus is squeezed out of his life. Then, and only then, will the wet blanket brigade determine that he is ready to step out and serve God, in full submission to the rules and principles of their denomination, of course.

Many passionate followers of Christ have ended up missing the ministry that God has called them to. The wet blanket throwers, meanwhile, congratulate one another that they managed to "save" another young Christian from stepping out of line. They have made another disciple in their own image. The wet blanket brigade believes they are doing God a service, when in fact they have become instruments of Satan. Jesus sternly warned the Pharisees with these chilling words: "Woe to you, teachers of the law and Pharisees, you hypocrites! You travel over land and sea to win a single convert, and when he becomes one, you make him twice as much a son of hell as you are" (Matt. 23:15).

Such a barren spiritual environment is destructive to God's people. A church like this will never experience the presence of God in their midst until they repent and stop trying to control others. The wet blanket brigade needs to get out of the way and realize that Jesus is the Good Shepherd and is more than able to take care of His flock!

In China the church used to be somewhat similar to the church in many parts of the Western world today. There were few salvations, and the land was riddled with dozens of competing Christian sects and denominations. By God's mercy, after the arrival of Communism in 1949, these man-made traditions and denominational walls came crashing down as the church experienced decades of harsh persecution. These experiences purified and simplified the body of Christ in China, leaving us without any structures to depend on. Instead, men and women, boys and girls everywhere started to depend on Jesus Christ. Now that the stifling confines of religious walls had been removed, the gospel spread freely and rapidly. Many were moved by the Holy Spirit to go and share the good news throughout the nation, and nobody tried to throw a wet blanket over them. Instead, they were encouraged and sent forth with the blessings and prayers of the whole church. They were willing to die for the gospel if necessary, and many experienced torture, imprisonment and severe hardship for the sake of the kingdom of God. These persecutions were received with thanks by those who were afflicted. They continued on their way, "rejoicing because they had been counted worthy of suffering disgrace for the Name" (Acts 5:41).

We did not have seminaries or organized Bible schools to go to, so we trusted the Lord Jesus instead. His Word became precious to us, and we learned to trust God for every single thing we needed. He never failed us. In later years some Western pastors visited China and asked us what seminary we attended and what materials we used. We replied, "Many of us have attended the Holy Spirit Devotional Bible School [meaning prison], and our only materials were the foot chains that bound us and the leather whips that bruised us."

When you begin to step out and serve the Lord, you will no doubt realize that your actions may bring opposition from the lost people and communities you go to share the gospel with. When Jesus sent out His first seventy-two disciples in pairs, they returned with great joy and reported, "Lord, even the demons submit to us in your name." Jesus replied, "I saw Satan fall like lightning from heaven" (Luke 10:17–18). You can be sure that whenever you proclaim the good news of Jesus Christ, Satan will strongly oppose you in any way he can. But when the kingdom of God is proclaimed and demonstrated with the power of the Holy Spirit, Satan will be bound and his plans will fail.

In my personal experience, I have found that whenever I step out in obedience to do something that God told me to do, all hell breaks loose. Fiery darts come raining down from every direction. The Back to Jerusalem vision is a good example. Satan has opposed this, as he doesn't want to see his kingdom collapse in those parts of the world where the gospel has not yet shone. Satan holds billions of people captive and intends to drag them to hell for eternity. For countless centuries he has tightly controlled these regions and people groups, and he will not give them up without a fierce fight. Most of us are aware that these kinds of attacks come on all who seek to reach the lost.

In God's kingdom there is no need for a wet blanket brigade. Instead, our heavenly Father wants people ready and willing to bring in His harvest of souls in these last days.

In my life, there have been times when all kinds of attacks came against me through newspapers, magazines, the Internet and even television reports. I didn't know much about these modern communication tools, but I know that God allows these attacks to come against me to make my faith stronger and the fire in my heart burn more brightly. I thank God for giving me this opportunity to grow in faith. Unless the Lord allows it, my enemies have no chance of pouring water over me. They cannot quench the fire of God in me, and I have seen how Jesus has turned the water into oil, and many more lost people have been brought into God's family as a result.

If you desire to truly serve God, you will be attacked. This is certain. But if your motivation is to do God's will and to carry out the Great Commission, you can advance without fear. The attacks will cause you to examine your motives, and God will search your heart to see if your service for Him is valid. If a person's motivation is not pure, everything he does will fail.

I would like to talk about another kind of attack the enemy orchestrates against us. In recent years, soldiers have used a new expression to describe being killed or wounded by their own side. The worst insult a soldier can experience is to be wounded by "friendly fire". It is a terrible feeling to be shot by fellow soldiers whom you thought were on your side!

Unfortunately and tragically, "friendly fire" is alive and well among God's people today. To come under fire from fellow Christians, who are meant to be fighting on your side, is a miserable experience to have to cope with. Some Christians assume the worst about people they know nothing about. If there is a new preacher going around with a message worth listening to, assumptions about his motives and integrity are often made, such as, "He must be in it for the money," or "He is deceiving people with his false message."

How sad and grievous this is to the Holy Spirit!

Although the term "friendly fire" may be relatively new, sadly it has been practiced among believers since the church was birthed in the book of Acts. All throughout Christian history we can find instances of God's revival fire being quenched by church leaders, many of whom did so out of ignorance and a misguided belief that they were "protecting" the gospel. More often than not, however, they were persecuting that which they didn't understand.

When people and institutions don't receive us, we should remember that Jesus was also widely rejected by those whom He loved. When Jesus was born, the town of Bethlehem refused to open its doors to Him, and the Creator of the universe ended up being born in a stable surrounded by the stench of animal waste. When Jesus was just two years old, King Herod attempted to murder Him, but His parents took Him to Egypt after being warned by an angel. Jesus and His parents became refugees, fleeing for their lives from a brutal dictator.

When Jesus commenced His ministry, His own people, the Jews, rejected Him. John records that "he was in the world, and though the world was made through him, the world did not recognize him. He came to that which was his own, but his own did not receive him" (John 1:10–11).

Jesus' hometown, Nazareth, also rejected the King of Kings. After receiving a poor reaction when He taught at the synagogue, Jesus declared, "'Only in his hometown, among his relatives and in his own house is a prophet without honor.' He could not do any miracles there, except lay his hands on a few sick people and heal them. And he was amazed at their lack of faith" (Mark 6:4–6).

In the end, Jesus was condemned to death and crucified by those who preferred the company of a condemned murderer. What a bizarre irony it is that the almighty God, in human form, was rejected and scorned by His creation! Isaiah's depiction of the Messiah revealed that He would be "despised and rejected by men, a man of sorrows, and familiar with suffering. Like one from whom men hide their faces he was despised, and we esteemed him not" (Isa. 53:3).

If you are rejected by people because you belong to Jesus, then rejoice that you are walking in His footsteps. If you continue to obey what the Lord is telling you, don't be surprised if you soon find yourself an outcast. Your zeal and very presence may become too much for some people's consciences, and to ease their agitation, they will find it most convenient to push you away.

When other believers reject you and start circulating false reports about you, realize who is really behind all attacks against the children of God. For "our struggle is not against flesh and blood, but against the rulers, against the authorities, against the powers of this dark world and against the spiritual forces of evil in the heavenly realms" (Eph. 6:12).

When we come under such attack, we need to know who we are in Christ, and we need to know the one we are serving. We must focus our eyes on the goal to which God has called us and not allow the attacks of the enemy to take us off the path on which we are called to walk. The apostle Paul had his share of attacks. The Scriptures offer a glimpse into what he endured for the name of Jesus Christ. When the Lord told Ananias to go and pray for Paul, he was told, "Go! This man is my chosen instrument to carry my name before the Gentiles and their kings and before the people of Israel. I will show him how much he must suffer for my name" (Acts 9:15–16). We know that Paul did suffer greatly for the name of Jesus, even being dragged into the arena in Ephesus and made to fight against wild beasts (see 1 Cor. 15:32).

How was it that Paul was able to continue on, buffeted but not defeated by the countless attacks and slanders against him? The answer is found in his words to Timothy: "I have fought the good fight, I have finished the race, I have kept the faith. Now there is in store for me the crown of righteousness, which the Lord, the righteous Judge, will award to me on that day—and not only to me, but also to all who have longed for his appearing" (2 Tim. 4:7–8).

Paul's heart was not focused on this life, for if it was, he would have been crushed by all the hardship he had to face. Rather, the apostle was focused on eternity, and he received grace to endure. Paul knew his troubles in this life were temporary and would soon be over. The secret to his endurance can be found in these words he wrote to the believers in Corinth: "We do not lose heart. Though outwardly we are wasting away, yet inwardly we are being renewed day by day. For our light and momentary troubles are achieving for us an eternal glory that far outweighs them all. So we fix our eyes not on what is seen, but on what is unseen. For what is seen is temporary, but what is unseen is eternal" (2 Cor. 4:16–18).

The Lord Jesus also endured intense trials by looking past the here and now and focusing on the future. The Bible exhorts us to follow His example: "Let us fix our eyes on Jesus, the author and perfecter of our faith, who for the joy set before him endured the cross, scorning its shame, and sat down at the right hand of the throne of God. Consider him who endured such opposition from sinful men, so that you will not grow weary and lose heart" (Heb. 12:2–3).

Have you ever been on a long boat voyage? If you are susceptible to seasickness, you may dread every moment of the journey, but after you arrive safely at your destination, you soon forget about the choppy seas. The joy of seeing the faces of your friends more than compensates for the difficulties you experienced. In the same way, when we reach heaven, we will soon forget all the struggles and difficulties of the journey through this life.

Every time I get discouraged, I stop and remember that one day I will run into the glory of God, and the Lord with His saints will warmly welcome me to my heavenly dwelling. "For while we are in this tent, we groan and are burdened, because we do not wish to be unclothed but to be clothed with our heavenly dwelling, so that what is mortal may be swallowed up by life" (2 Cor. 5:4).

Every Christian I know who has obeyed the call of God has been opposed both by the world and by other members of the body of Christ. How blind we can be! We cannot fight both the kingdom of darkness and each other at the same time. Satan knows that if he can turn Christian against Christian, he has already won the battle. Paul pointed this out to feuding believers long ago when he wrote, "The very fact that you have lawsuits among you means you have been completely defeated already" (1 Cor. 6:7).

There are too many quarrels between Christians today. We are quick to point out the faults of our brothers and sisters, but the Bible reveals that we need to look at our own lives. James asked, "What causes fights and quarrels among you? Don't they come from your desires that battle within you? You want something but don't get it. You kill and covet, but you cannot have what you want. You quarrel and fight. You do not have, because you do not ask God" (James 4:1–2).

Jesus warned His followers against having a critical and judgmental spirit. If we all took heed of His words, the church would be much more effective: "Why do you look at the speck of sawdust in your brother's eye and pay no attention to the plank in your own eye? How can you say to your brother, 'Let me take the speck out of your eye,' when all the time there is a plank in your own eye? You hypocrite, first take the plank out of your own eye, and then you will see clearly to remove the speck from your brother's eye" (Matt. 7:3–5).

We need to completely forgive those who attack, accuse and criticize us unfairly. Don't hold any bitterness toward them, for this will only lead to your own destruction. Bitterness is the Devil's often-used strategy to distract Christians from God's work and to stunt their usefulness for God's kingdom. God is able to take all the "friendly fire" people throw at us and use it to build more character into our lives.

When people try to discourage and slander you or spread all kinds of false accusations about you, don't listen to them! Have your heart set on Jesus and His kingdom, realizing that "in all these things we are more than conquerors through him who loved us" (Rom. 8:37). Jesus clearly told us the way we should respond in such circumstances: "Blessed are you when people insult you, persecute you and falsely say all kinds of evil against you because of me. Rejoice and be glad, because great is your reward in heaven, for in the same way they persecuted the prophets who were before you" (Matt. 5:11–12).

We thank God for the many wonderful Christians around the world who have heard about the Back to Jerusalem vision of the Chinese church to take the gospel to the Muslim, Hindu and Buddhist peoples. We are constantly amazed at how people contact us enthusiastically, saying they want to be a part of this vision. Not everyone is enamored by the thought of Chinese believers going as missionaries outside our borders, however. Even some so-called mission leaders have written that the vision is nonsense and will never take place. They are so blind that they don't realize it is already taking place!

Since the Back to Jerusalem vision started to grow, many people have spoken bad words against us. The enemy has caused many people to personally attack me. This reached a crescendo of quite ridiculous proportions, and few of the critics really want to hear the truth. They are just happy to jump on the bandwagon and attack those things they cannot control.

As the attacks against us increased, I did not feel too discouraged. Rather, I came to the realization that the Back to Jerusalem vision really must be something very close to the heart of God; otherwise Satan would never try so hard to destroy it! During one meeting in Europe, a mature Christian approached me and said, "Brother Yun, I didn't know anything about you, but when I started to hear all the nasty accusations and rumors about how rotten you are, I was astounded. I realized that for Satan to go out of his way and deceive so many key Christian leaders to denounce and attack you, you must pose a threat to the kingdom of darkness. When I heard that even the Chinese government was trying to destroy your reputation, I understood that you must be a kingdom-minded person. Otherwise, it made no sense why these people would waste so much time and energy to attack you."

These critics do not understand that Back to Jerusalem is not something that anyone can control. No denomination, church or mission organization can control it. It is a vision given by God to the whole church in this generation. God is not interested in "our" work or "our" ministry at all. It is vitally important for all who serve God to examine whether they really exist to serve the kingdom of God and the whole body of Christ or whether they exist just to serve their own interests and to protect their own "turf". Such ministries are doomed to failure, for the enabling power of the Holy Spirit will be absent, and all their work will be done with mere human effort.

A ministry should not even exist, for example, to serve the church in China. This might sound admirable on the surface, but it is not right. Your ministry should exist to serve God's kingdom purposes and to glorify Him alone. This is what I have attempted to preach everywhere I have gone, but many people whose energies are focused primarily on protecting their own achievements feel threatened by such a message. Some are aghast that we share the Back to Jerusalem vision to send thousands of Chinese missionaries out of China. They feel that this message damages "their" ministry because they are still trying to send missionaries *into* China!

Jesus did not come and die on the cross to help failing ministries be restored. He didn't come so you could receive a comfortable salary and be respected by the members of your congregation. No! He came so that God's rule and authority would be rightfully expanded throughout all parts of the sin-stained world.

I don't care what agendas and objectives all the other ministries and organizations in this world may have. My sole concern is that we would remain kingdom-minded and kingdom-guided servants, so that even those who operate their ministries on their own would be challenged to join hands with us in advancing the kingdom of God throughout the earth.

If you want to be a kingdom-minded person, you will quickly become a threat to Satan and the kingdom of darkness. All kinds of attacks will come falling down on you like poisonous arrows. Brothers and sisters, it is not about us. Don't look to any man or man-made institution. Look to our heavenly Father alone. He is able to protect you from all harm.

When the king of Assyria came to attack God's people, Hezekiah stood and declared, "Be strong and courageous. Do not be afraid or discouraged because of the king of Assyria and the vast army with him, for there is a greater power with us than with him. With him is only the arm of flesh, but with us is the LORD our God to help us and to fight our battles" (2 Chron. 32:7–8). Those who attack us for no reason have only the arm of the flesh, but we have the Lord Jesus Christ.

May the Lord help us to walk in the camp of those who belong to Him, and may we never fall into the deception of thinking that Christian work is about us and our own desires and plans. Oh Lord, please make us kingdom-minded followers. Give us a revelation that we are not called to *build* Your kingdom, but You will *bring* Your kingdom. Amen.

27

Giant Slayers

> For this purpose the Son of God was manifested, that
> he might destroy the works of the devil.
>
> *1 John 3:8 KJV*

*I*n order to see what God is doing today, we must cultivate a close intimate relationship with Jesus Christ and view things from God's perspective. Even if we see a giant standing before us, we should not be intimidated. The giant might be real, but Jesus Christ is the Truth who can bring peace and freedom to any situation. Even when we are struggling, we should stop and meditate on the fact that Jesus has purchased us as His own possession. To do so, He paid the highest price—His own life. Those who have been born again into God's kingdom now belong to Jesus. They are inseparable, to such an extent that the Bible says, "If we are faithless, he will remain faithful, for he cannot disown himself" (2 Tim. 2:13).

What a marvelous exchange we have been privileged to partake in! We can bring our dirty rags to the cross and exchange them for robes of righteousness. The prophet Zechariah had a vision in which he saw an exchange between the high priest, Joshua, and an angel. Joshua "was dressed in filthy clothes as he stood before the angel. The angel said to those who were standing before him, 'Take off his filthy clothes.' Then he said to Joshua, 'See, I have taken away your sin, and I will put rich garments on you.' Then I said, 'Put a clean turban on his head.' So they put a clean turban on his head and clothed him, while the angel of the LORD stood by" (Zech. 3:3–5).

We can give God our sins in exchange for forgiveness and a new life. What a good and gracious God we serve! It is amazing to me that everyone in the world doesn't immediately respond to Jesus and follow Him wholeheartedly!

As we begin to serve our Savior, we need to understand that God's work must be done God's way. We must rely on His wisdom alone and not on man's wisdom, "For the foolishness of God is wiser than man's wisdom, and the weakness of God is stronger than man's strength" (1 Cor. 1:25). As you serve God, you will surely experience much opposition. When this happens you need to know who you are, who you are not, who is the enemy you are facing and who is the Lord you are serving.

If you have been saved and restored into right relationship with God, then you should never accept the taunts of the enemy. When the enemy mocks and attempts to intimidate you, it is imperative that you stand up in the authority of Jesus Christ and refuse to accept it!

Let us consider the story of David and Goliath. The first thing to note is that Goliath's very appearance caused fear. The Bible paints the following dramatic picture: "He was over nine feet tall. He had a bronze helmet on his head and wore a coat of scale armor of bronze weighing five thousand shekels; on his legs he wore bronze greaves, and a bronze javelin was slung on his back. His spear shaft was like a weaver's rod, and its iron point weighed six hundred shekels. His shield bearer went ahead of him" (1 Sam. 17:4–7).

The enemy always tries to scare God's people and cause them to become incapacitated by fear. For forty long days Goliath stood up and threatened the Israelites. His threats achieved their purpose, for the Bible records that "on hearing the Philistine's words, Saul and all the Israelites were dismayed and terrified" (1 Sam. 17:11).

Remember that "the foolishness of God is wiser than man's wisdom, and the weakness of God is stronger than man's strength" (1 Cor. 1:25). God chose to respond to this threat not by sending one of Israel's great warriors to fight Goliath, nor even by cutting the giant down by divine intervention. Rather, God chose a young boy named David–the youngest of eight brothers–to destroy the enemy and silence their blasphemies.

On the morning of the fortieth consecutive day, Goliath came out and mocked the people of God. By this time the whole of the Israelite army had been thoroughly terrorized and traumatized to such an extent that "when the Israelites saw the man, they all ran from him in great fear" (1 Sam. 17:24). On this particular day, however, young David happened to be visiting the camp and heard Goliath's words for himself. Something stirred deep within his spirit, and he asked, "Who is this uncircumcised Philistine that he should defy the armies of the living God?" (17:26).

Together, we are the armies of the living God today. We are the armies of Jesus Christ. The Lord God calls all of His children to fight in His name, but many fall prey to fear and intimidation. If they manage to overcome their fears, the Devil uses different strategies in a bid to disarm and cripple the obedient Christian.

One of his favorite tactics is to cause other believers to bring discouragement. This is what happened to David. His oldest brother, Eliab, "burned with anger at him and asked, 'Why have you come down here? And with whom did you leave those few sheep in the desert? I know how conceited you are and how wicked your heart is; you came down only to watch the battle'" (1 Sam. 17:28).

Isn't it strange that Eliab would "burn with anger" just because his brother showed more courage than he did? Eliab also resorted to slander in order to keep his young brother in line, even telling David, "I know how conceited you are and how wicked your heart is; you came down only to watch the battle." Satan often uses family members to bring discouragement. The closer the person is to you, the more crippling their discouragement is. This is often what happens in the church today, as our own brothers and sisters in the Lord end up trying to prevent us from following what God has told us to do.

When people try to stop you or spread all kinds of false reports about you, don't listen to them! Be like David, and pay them no attention. It reveals much of David's heart that even though he was just a young boy, he refused to be affected by his brother's discouragement. In fact, David approached King Saul and boldly announced, "Let no one lose heart on account of this Philistine; your servant will go and fight him" (1 Sam. 17:32).

Another interesting thing happened before David slew Goliath. Before he went out to meet the giant, "Saul dressed David in his own tunic. He put a coat of armor on him and a bronze helmet on his head. David fastened on his sword over the tunic and tried walking around, because he was not used to them. 'I cannot go in these,' he said to Saul, 'because I am not used to them.' So he took them off. Then he took his staff in his hand, chose five smooth stones from the stream, put them in the pouch of his shepherd's bag and, with his sling in his hand, approached the Philistine" (1 Sam. 17:38–40).

Many well-meaning believers will try to help you as you serve God by trying to add human weapons to your battle equipment. Many people have come to us in China and tried to fit a helmet on our heads and armor on our bodies. They have said, "Dear brother, these have been used many times before, and they will help you in the battle." These things can take many forms, be they some training course that someone insists you should do or a certain method that you should use. Some brothers have suggested that the Christians in China should not consider being missionaries in other countries because we are not "qualified". Few of us have university degrees, nor have we ever graduated from one of their seminaries.

While there is nothing wrong with Christians having a university degree if that is the way God led them, to try to impose this requirement on someone is ridiculous and will only serve to hinder the person as they follow Christ. If this happens to you, I encourage you to be like David and take off the expectation, because you are "not used to [it]".

David was used to a simple life as a shepherd. He was familiar with using a sling and had killed both a lion and a bear while protecting his sheep. Don't try to be someone God didn't make you. It will just be awkward and diminish your effectiveness for the Lord.

I believe God would not allow David to go into battle with Saul's armor and weapons, as people might have been tempted to credit David's success to the equipment he was wearing rather than to the Lord God alone. It is our all-powerful, all-knowing

Sovereign who has declared, "How can I let myself be defamed? I will not yield my glory to another" (Isa. 48:11).

After David killed Goliath, news of what happened quickly spread to the surrounding nations, and there was no mistaking the fact that God had provided the victory. David had declared to the Philistine, "You come against me with sword and spear and javelin, but I come against you in the name of the LORD Almighty, the God of the armies of Israel, whom you have defied. This day the LORD will hand you over to me, and I'll strike you down and cut off your head. Today I will give the carcasses of the Philistine army to the birds of the air and the beasts of the earth, and the whole world will know that there is a God in Israel. All those gathered here will know that it is not by sword or spear that the LORD saves; for the battle is the LORD's, and he will give all of you into our hands" (1 Sam. 17:45–47).

When you have a vision that can be accomplished without God's help, then you will receive the glory when it is completed. If you have a vision that is absolutely impossible unless God intervenes, He alone will receive the glory and praise. I encourage you to ask the Lord to use your life in ways that bring maximum glory to His name and the greatest benefit for His kingdom.

Having ignored all of the critics and faithless men around him, David pressed forward, with the glory of God foremost on his mind. The cowering Israelites must have watched on in amazement as David actually "ran quickly toward the battle line to meet him" (1 Sam. 17:48).

God gave a great victory, and David cut off Goliath's head. Have you ever noticed what happened next? The Bible says, "When the Philistines saw that their hero was dead, they turned and ran. Then the men of Israel and Judah surged forward with a shout and pursued the Philistines to the entrance of Gath and to the gates of Ekron. Their dead were strewn along the Shaaraim road to Gath and Ekron" (17:51–52).

Just minutes earlier the Israelite soldiers had considered the prospect of beating Goliath to be impossible and had been terrorized by his taunts and blasphemies. Now the impossible had happened, and their perspective experienced a dramatic shift. One bold act of faith in the kingdom of God can result in a flood of believers experiencing a breakthrough into a new freedom and sense of victory.

Once when I was in a prison labor camp in China, I was appointed shepherd of the sheep that grazed within the prison's land. I tried all I could to get the sheep to follow me, but nothing worked. Finally, I discovered that if I picked up the smallest lamb and carried it, then all the other sheep would follow.

Sometimes the Lord allows us to become like that weak lamb. Then if we allow Him to carry us, it can become an opportunity for many people to follow. This is what happened when God chose David to slay the giant, and this is what continues to happen in numerous different ways throughout the world today. God's kingdom advances when the almighty God uses weak men and women, and not through human strength and bravado.

Finally, the story of David and Goliath concludes with these words: "When the Israelites returned from chasing the Philistines, they plundered their camp. David took the Philistine's head and brought it to Jerusalem, and he put the Philistine's weapons in his own tent" (1 Sam. 17:53–54).

Does it sound a little strange that David would reject Saul's weapons, yet he didn't hesitate to take Goliath's head and weapons as souvenirs?

It should come as no surprise, for David had disarmed the enemy. This is what all of God's people are called to do. The apostle Paul said of the Lord Jesus, "Having disarmed principalities and powers, He made a public spectacle of them, triumphing over them in it" (Col. 2:15 NKJV). This was the great privilege of David, and this is the great privilege of Jesus' disciples today.

The Lord is looking for more giant slayers today. He is not pleased when those who are called by His name hide themselves and remain silent as evil voices loudly blaspheme God. Our Father is looking for people who, like David, will bravely stand up and fight for His kingdom.

Will you be a David to this generation?

28

Wait upon the Lord

I wait for the LORD, my soul waits, and in his word I put my hope. My soul waits for the Lord more than watchmen wait for the morning.

Psalm 130:5–6

Be still before the LORD and wait patiently for him; do not fret when men succeed in their ways, when they carry out their wicked schemes.

Psalm 37:7

Chinese Christians believe the Scriptures are the unchangeable Word of God, so Bibles are very precious to us. In the 1970s – after more than two decades of persecution – there was a great shortage of Bibles in the land. We were starving for God's Word, as in the days spoken of by the prophet Amos:

"The days are coming," declares the Sovereign LORD, "when I will send a famine through the land – not a famine of food or a thirst for water, but a famine of hearing the words of the LORD. Men will stagger from sea to sea and wander from north to east, searching for the word of the LORD, but they will not find it."

Amos 8:11–12

Many believers in the past were buried with their Bibles inside their coffins, and we were so desperate for God's Word that many graves were dug up in order to retrieve what we could of the precious Bible. In most cases the paper had been worn away by moisture and time, but the opportunity to recover even half a page of God's Word was worth the effort. Other Christians lovingly placed their Bibles inside clay pots and buried them deep in the ground. Years later, when the persecution eased, they dug them up again.

After I first met the Lord in 1974, I was so eager to read God's Word that I prayed and fasted for 100 days, eating just one small bowl of rice a day. My parents thought I was losing my mind because of desperation and despair, but finally the Lord miraculously provided a Bible for me.

Now that I have explained my love and respect for the Word of God, let me make a statement that might seem contradictory at first glance. As I have traveled to various nations, I have come to see that some Christians think if they can just receive better Bible teaching, then everything will fall into place and their churches will be strong again. I believe this is *not* the most important thing that you need. Let me digress by repeating that I love the Word of God, have memorized whole books of the Bible and appreciate good teaching as much as anyone.

But Bible teaching, in itself, will not change your lives and churches. What you need most is the presence of the Holy Spirit! Bible knowledge may be like a reservoir of oil in your life, but without the flame of the Holy Spirit, your oil will not provide light and warmth to people who need to know Jesus.

The disciples were with Jesus for three and a half years, every day and night. They received the greatest Bible teaching in the history of the world, for Jesus did not just teach the

Word of God; He *is* the Word of God in human form! The disciples not only heard the Bible being taught; they saw it demonstrated every day.

The disciples had already been told that they would preach the good news throughout the world (see Matt. 24:14), yet after Jesus was crucified and resurrected, a strange thing happened to the disciples. Jesus had told them to return to Galilee, where He would meet them on a mountain. When the risen Lord appeared there, however, he found six of the disciples out fishing on the Sea of Galilee (see John 21:1–14). They had been unable to catch a single fish before Jesus arrived and guided their efforts. All of a sudden, after Jesus became involved, their nets filled with 153 large fish!

I have often wondered why these disciples were busy fishing when Jesus had told them to proclaim the gospel to people. I have come to this conclusion: The disciples were not lacking Bible teaching, vision or understanding. They were, however, lacking the Holy Spirit!

It wasn't until the disciples were all baptized by the Holy Spirit on the day of Pentecost that they became flames of fire for God's kingdom. Men who had been nervous and weak all of a sudden became as bold as lions. Thomas, who doubted that Jesus had been raised from the dead, was mightily transformed into a missionary who traveled to India and established the first churches there before dying as a martyr. The disciples, who had felt abandoned and confused a short time earlier, performed miracles and signs and wonders everywhere they went. Peter, who had denied the Lord three times, was given the honor of preaching the gospel on the day of Pentecost, and 3,000 people gave their lives to Jesus!

The difference in their lives was not Bible teaching, but the Holy Spirit!

He provided the flame, and the oil began to burn powerfully. The light of the gospel shone into the darkness, and the darkness could not snuff it out. Like moths, thousands of people were attracted to the light, and the church grew quickly. The Bible says, "Every day they continued to meet together in the temple courts. They broke bread in their homes and ate together with glad and sincere hearts, praising God and enjoying the favor of all the people. And the Lord added to their number daily those who were being saved" (Acts 2:46–47). Within weeks, about 5,000 men in Jerusalem had put their trust in Jesus Christ (4:4).

The revival was so intense that "more and more men and women believed in the Lord and were added to their number. As a result, people brought the sick into the streets and laid them on beds and mats so that at least Peter's shadow might fall on some of them as he passed by. Crowds gathered also from the towns around Jerusalem, bringing their sick and those tormented by evil spirits, and all of them were healed" (Acts 5:14–16).

What a shock all those Pharisees and teachers of the law must have felt! Just weeks before, they had rejoiced as Jesus was crucified. Now that they had got Him out of the way, they surely felt His teaching would drift away and things would soon return to "normal" in Jerusalem. Instead, the whole city was abuzz with Jesus, and He was the centerpiece of all conversations throughout the country. The authorities responded by persecuting the believers, but this only had the effect of adding fuel to the flames, and the good news spread even further. Luke records, "So the word of God spread. The number of disciples in Jerusalem increased rapidly, and a large number of priests became obedient to the faith" (Acts 6:7).

Satan and his demonic forces must have been terrified by what was happening. What they thought was their greatest victory—the killing of God's Son—had turned into their biggest nightmare and signaled their defeat. Paul wrote that Jesus, "having disarmed the powers and authorities, made a public spectacle of them, triumphing over them by the cross" (Col. 2:15). No wonder the Bible says, "None of the rulers of this age understood it, for if they had, they would not have crucified the Lord of glory" (1 Cor. 2:8).

The disciples were told to wait for the Holy Spirit, and we too must wait upon the Lord as we serve Him. It is foolish and dangerous to run ahead of His perfect timing. In many places the Bible instructs us to wait: "Wait for the LORD; be strong and take heart and wait for the LORD" (Ps. 27:14); "Be still before the LORD and wait patiently for him" (Ps. 37:7); "But as for me, I watch in hope for the LORD, I wait for God my Savior; my God will hear me" (Mic. 7:7).

If you feel tired and worn out in your Christian life, then you also should wait upon the Lord. This doesn't mean just sit there and do nothing. It means spending time pouring your heart out to God, feeding on His Word and waiting for Him to take your weakness and exchange it with His mighty strength. For our Lord "gives strength to the weary and increases the power of the weak. Even youths grow tired and weary, and young men stumble and fall; but those who hope in the LORD will renew their strength. They will soar on wings like eagles; they will run and not grow weary, they will walk and not be faint" (Isa. 40:29–31).

Brothers and sisters, have you ever been filled with the Holy

Spirit like the disciples? Does God's mighty Spirit overflow your whole being, transforming you and everyone around you? Or have you settled for acquiring knowledge, as you trudge along through life, hoping to make it to the finish line with your faith intact?

I believe with all my heart that God wants you to be filled with the Holy Spirit so that streams of living water will flow from within you.

God wants the heavy anchors you have created for your faith to be hoisted up so that the wind of the Holy Spirit can blow on you and cause you to move!

I'm telling you from personal experience that when God's people are filled with the Holy Spirit, they are never the same again. You won't have to try to find ways to get people to come to your meetings, for they will beat a path to your door and beg you to tell them how they might be saved. In China we have experienced such an outpouring of God's presence and power that on some occasions the local authorities have been gripped by the fear of God and have refused to persecute us in any way, afraid that God will judge them if they raise a finger against His children.

When people are not full of God's Spirit, human introductions are so important in the church. People say, "Here is a brother who has done this and that for the Lord, and I recommend him to you." Everything is so prim and proper. But when God's power comes through His kingdom, you will not need any human introductions to preach the gospel! When God's flame is inside a person, everyone will know it. Those who are on the side of the Lord will welcome it, while others will attack it and try to quench the flame.

When the Holy Spirit is absent, people become so important.

Believers look to preachers with big names and flock to meetings where someone has a new kind of message. But when the Holy Spirit is present, nobody cares about who is preaching, or anybody's name, because all are concerned only about glorifying Jesus and making His name great!

If you are a follower of Jesus Christ, then don't be afraid. The Prince of Peace lives in your heart, and you should not be scared of anything. If God is for you, no one and nothing can be against you. Ask God to fill you with the Holy Spirit, and you will never be the same again!

When I was invited to speak in Israel, I was very excited. My hosts graciously took me around many places, showing me various biblical ruins, tunnels, valleys and hills. These were all interesting, but I quickly realized that Jesus wasn't in any of these historical places. Rather, He is alive in my heart!

His power and life reside in my heart, here and now! And He resides in the hearts of all who believe in Him.

Time is short, and it is valuable. Don't waste any more time trying to serve God in your own strength and with your own ideas.

Jesus is alive!

Stop living like He is dead.

Let the living Jesus shine from your life. There is no reason to go around with a sour face! Turn your mourning into dancing and your sorrow into joy.

If you are a pastor, don't go home and pull out all your old notes from seminary. Please don't offer old lukewarm, stagnant water to your flock. They will just get diarrhea and the people will be running to the toilet for the rest of their lives! They don't need your regurgitated teachings. They need the living water of the Holy Spirit!

For those preachers who rely on old notes or other people's thoughts to get sermons, I encourage you to go home, take out your notes and make a burnt offering to the Lord! Just as the manna that fell from heaven was fresh only for that day, you also must have fresh messages for God's people, the overflow of an intimate relationship with Jesus Christ. Regarding the manna, Moses told the Israelites, "'No one is to keep any of it until morning.' However, some of them paid no attention to Moses; they kept part of it until morning, but it was full of maggots and began to smell. So Moses was angry with them" (Ex. 16:19–20). God's people need fresh heavenly food to nourish their hungry hearts.

When the Holy Spirit fills you, you can achieve more of eternal worth in a moment than in years of your own striving. That is what Peter and the other apostles experienced after Pentecost, and it is also the experience of millions of God's servants around the world since.

How can you be filled with the Holy Spirit?

It's quite simple. Fall on your knees and ask God to release you from your prison of dead religion and to overflow you with His real and vibrant presence! Jesus taught, "Ask and it will be given to you; seek and you will find; knock and the door will be opened to you. For everyone who asks receives; he who seeks finds; and to him who knocks, the door will be opened. Which of you fathers, if your son asks for a fish, will give him a snake instead? Or if he asks for an egg, will give him a scorpion? If you then, though you are evil, know how to give good gifts to your children, how much more will your Father in heaven give the Holy Spirit to those who ask him!" (Luke 11:9–13).

Our God is a good and loving Father, and He desires to fill you with the Holy Spirit. Not only does He want to fill you, but He wants streams of living water to overflow and bless those with whom you come into contact.

This is what some people call "ministry."

" 'If anyone is thirsty, let him come to me and drink. Whoever believes in me, as the Scripture has said, streams of living water will flow from within him.' By this he meant the Spirit, whom those who believed in him were later to receive" (John 7:37–39).

You will never be the same again.

Contact Information

You can receive the latest information on Brother Yun, updates on the Chinese house churches and the Back to Jerusalem movement and ways to pray for and support the advance of the gospel by the Chinese church by logging on to this website: www.backtojerusalem.com.

Paul Hattaway is a New Zealand–born missionary who has authored many books about the church in Asia, including the bestselling *The Heavenly Man*, *Back to Jerusalem*, *Operation China* and *China's Christian Martyrs*. Hattaway is also director of Asia Harvest, an interdenominational ministry that serves the church in China and around Asia through various strategic initiatives, including Bible printing in China and support of the families of persecuted believers. To receive the free Asia Harvest newsletter, go to www.asiaharvest.org, or write to the address below nearest you:

Asia Harvest
1903 60th Place, Ste M1204
Bradenton, FL 34203
UNITED STATES

Asia Harvest
Mill Farm
Fleetwood Road
Wesham, PR4 3HD
ENGLAND

Asia Harvest
36 Nelson Street
Stepney, SA 5069
AUSTRALIA

Asia Harvest
PO Box 181
Te Anau, 9640
NEW ZEALAND

Asia Harvest
Clementi Central PO Box 119
SINGAPORE 911204

Asia Harvest
PO Box 8036
Pejabat Pos Kelana Jaya
46780 Petaling Jaya
Selangor
MALAYSIA

THE HEAVENLY MAN

the remarkable true
story of Chinese Christian
Brother Yun

AS TOLD TO PAUL HATTAWAY

Humble Beginnings

My name is Liu Zhenying. My Christian friends call me Brother Yun.

One morning in autumn 1999, I awoke in the city of Bergen in western Norway. My heart was stirred and excitement bubbled up inside me. I had been speaking in churches throughout Scandinavia, testifying about the Chinese house churches and inviting Christians to join us as we evangelize all of China and the nations beyond. My hosts had asked me if I would like to visit the grave of Marie Monsen, a great Lutheran missionary to China who had been mightily used by God to revive the church in different parts of my nation from 1901 to 1932. Her ministry was especially effective in the southern part of Henan Province, where I come from.

Miss Monsen was small in stature, yet a giant in God's kingdom. The Chinese church was not only impacted by her words, but also deeply challenged by her sacrificial lifestyle. She was a fully committed, uncompromising follower of Jesus Christ, who showed us an example of how to suffer and endure for the Lord.

God used Marie Monsen in a powerful manner, so that many miracles, signs and wonders followed her ministry. She returned to Norway in 1932 to take care of her elderly parents, and by then her work in China was complete. She never returned to China, but her legacy of uncompromising faith, unquenchable zeal and the necessity of changed hearts fully committed to the cause of Christ lives on in the Chinese church today.

Now I had the great privilege of visiting her grave in her homeland. I wondered if any other Chinese Christian had ever enjoyed the privilege I was about to enjoy. When she came to our part of China there were few Christians and the church was weak. Today there are millions of believers. On their behalf I planned to offer thanks to God for her life.

Our car pulled up at the graveyard, situated on the side of a hill in a narrow valley, with a river flowing through it. We walked around for a few minutes, hoping to see her name on one of the several hundred tombstones. Not being able to locate Monsen's grave immediately, we strolled to the office for help. The administrator was not familiar with her name, so he looked in a book that lists the names of the dead who are buried there. After flicking through the pages he told us some news I found hard to believe, "Marie Monsen was indeed buried here in 1962. But her grave was left untended for many years, so today it is just an empty lot with no headstone."

In Chinese culture the memory of people who did great things is cherished for many generations to come, so I never imagined that such a thing could happen. The local believers explained that Marie Monsen was still held in high regard and that they had honoured her memory in different ways, such as by publishing her biography decades after she died. But to me her unmarked grave was an insult that had to be made right.

I was deeply grieved. With a heavy heart I sternly told the Norwegian Christians who were with me, "You must honour this woman of God! I will give you two years to construct a new grave and headstone in memory of Marie Monsen. If you fail to do this, I will personally arrange for some Christian brothers to walk all the way from China to Norway to build one! Many brothers in China are skilled stonecutters because of their years in prison labour camps for the sake of the gospel. If you don't care enough, they will be more than willing to do it!"

I was born in 1958, during the Chinese leap year – the fourth of five children in our family. I came into the world in an old traditional farming village named Liu Lao Zhuang in Nanyang County, in the southern part of China's Henan Province.

Henan contains almost 100 million souls – China's most populated province. Despite this fact, there seemed to be many open spaces where I grew up – lots of hills to scale and trees to climb. Although life was difficult, I also remember times of fun when I was a little boy.

All of the 600 people in our village were farmers, and still are to this day. Not too much has changed. We mostly cultivated potatoes, corn, and wheat. We also grew cabbages and other kinds of root vegetables.

Our home was a simple structure of compacted dried mud. The roof was made of straw. The rain always managed to find the holes in our roof, while in winter the icy winds never failed to blow through the gaps in our walls. When the temperatures dropped to below freezing we burned leftover corn husks to keep warm. We couldn't afford coal.

Often in the summer it was so hot and humid that we couldn't bear to sleep inside our poorly ventilated home.

Beds were dragged outside and our whole family joined the rest of the village sleeping in the cooler air.

"Henan" means "south of the river". The mighty Yellow River dissects the northern part of the province. Its frequent floods have brought centuries of pain to people living along its banks. We knew this as we grew up, but to us northern Henan was a million miles away.

Our village nestled in the hills of the southern part of the province, safe from devastating floods and outside influences. We were only concerned with the next harvest. Our lives completely revolved around the cycle of ploughing, planting, watering and harvesting. My dad always said it was a struggle just to get enough food to eat. All hands were required in the field, so from a young age I was called into action helping with my brothers and sisters. Consequently, I didn't have the opportunity to attend much school.

In other parts of China, Henan natives have a reputation for being as stubborn as donkeys. Perhaps it was that stubbornness that prevented the Henanese from receiving Christianity when Protestant missionaries first brought it to our province in 1884. Many missionaries laboured in Henan without much visible success. By 1922, after almost forty years of missionary effort, there were a mere 12,400 Protestant believers in the entire province.

Those who accepted the religion of the "foreign devils" were ridiculed and ostracized by their communities. Often the opposition spilled over into more violent expressions. Christians were beaten. Some were even killed for their faith. The missionaries, too, faced great persecution. Missionaries were considered by many people to be tools of imperialism and colonialism, sent by their nations to gain control over the hearts and minds of the Chinese people while their governments raped the land of its natural resources.

The outrage against foreigners reached its peak in 1900, when a secret society called "The Boxers" instigated a nationwide attack against foreigners. Most were able to flee the carnage, but many missionaries were located in remote rural areas of inland China, far from the safety of the large coastal cities. The Boxers brutally massacred more than 150 missionaries and thousands of their Chinese converts.

Those brave souls who had come to serve our nation sacrificially and bring the love of the Lord Jesus Christ to us were slaughtered. They had come to share Christ and to improve our lives by building hospitals, orphanages and schools. We repaid them with death.

In the aftermath, some people thought the events of 1900 would be enough to scare missionaries off ever coming back to China.

They were wrong.

On 1 September 1901, a large ship docked in Shanghai Port. A young single lady from Norway walked off the gangplank onto Chinese soil for the first time. Marie Monsen was one of a new wave of missionaries who, inspired by the martyrdoms of the previous year, had dedicated themselves to full-time missionary service in China.

Monsen stayed in China for more than thirty years. For a time she lived in my county, Nanyang, where she encouraged and trained a small group of Chinese believers that had sprung up.

Marie Monsen was different from most other missionaries. She didn't seem to be too concerned with making a good impression on the Chinese church leaders. She often told them, "You are all hypocrites! You confess Jesus Christ with your lips while your hearts are not fully committed to him! Repent before it is too late to escape God's judgment!" She brought fire from the altar of God.

Monsen told the Christians it wasn't enough to study the lives of born-again believers, but that they must themselves be radically born again in order to enter the kingdom of heaven. With such teaching, she took the emphasis off head knowledge and showed each individual that they were personally responsible before God for their own inner spiritual life. Hearts were convicted of sin and fires of revival swept throughout the villages of central China wherever she went.

In the 1940s another Western missionary preached the gospel to my mother, who was twenty years old at the time. Although she didn't fully understand, she was deeply impressed by what she heard. She especially liked to sing the songs and hear the Bible stories shared by the small teams of evangelists who travelled around the countryside. Soon she started attending church and committed her life to Jesus Christ.

China became a Communist nation in 1949. Within a few years all missionaries were expelled, church buildings were closed, and thousands of Chinese pastors were imprisoned. Many lost their lives. My mother saw the missionaries leave Nanyang in the early 1950s. She never forgot the tears in their eyes as they headed for the coast under armed guard, their ministries for the Lord having abruptly come to an end.

In just one city in China, Wenzhou in Zhejiang Province, 49 pastors were sent to prison labour camps near the Russian border in 1950. Many were given sentences of up to twenty years for their "crimes" of preaching the gospel. Of those 49 pastors, just one returned home. 48 died in prison.

In my home area of Nanyang, believers were crucified on

the walls of their churches for not denying Christ. Others were chained to vehicles and horses and dragged to their death.

One pastor was bound and attached to a long rope. The authorities, enraged that the man of God would not deny his faith, used a makeshift crane to lift him high into the air. Before hundreds of witnesses, who had come to accuse him falsely of being a "counter revolutionary", the pastor was asked one last time by his persecutors if he would recant. He shouted back, "No! I will never deny the Lord who saved me!" The rope was released and the pastor crashed to the ground below.

Upon inspection, the tormentors discovered the pastor was not fully dead, so they raised him up into the air for a second time, dropping the rope to finish him off for good. In this life the pastor was dead, but he lives on in heaven with the reward of one who was faithful to the end.

Life was not just difficult for Christians. Mao launched an experiment called the "Great Leap Forward", which led to a massive famine all over China. It was actually a great leap backwards for the nation. In my Henan Province it was estimated that 8 million people starved to death.

During these difficult times the small fiedgling church in my home town of Nanyang was scattered. They were like sheep without shepherds. My mother also left the church. Over the following decades, having been completely starved of all Christian fellowship and without God's Word, she forgot most of what she had learned as a young woman. Her relationship with the Lord grew cold.

*O*n 1 September 2001 – exactly one hundred years to the day since Marie Monsen first arrived in China to start her missionary career – more than three hundred Norwegian

Christians gathered in the Bergen graveyard for a special prayer and dedication ceremony. A beautiful new headstone was unveiled in memory of Monsen, paid for by contributions from various churches, and individual Christians.

Monsen's picture and her Chinese name appeared on the headstone, which also stated:

MARIE MONSEN 1878–1962 MISSIONARY IN CHINA 1901–1932

When I told the believers in China that Marie Monsen's gravestone had been rebuilt, they were thankful and relieved.

We must always be careful to remember the sacrifice of those God has used to establish his kingdom. They are worthy of our honour and respect.